The
Senior's Guide
to Easy Computing
HANDBOOK

Microsoft Windows XP, Vista, Windows 7 and Apple Mac OS X

**Check out these other great titles
by EKLEKTIKA Press:**

The Senior's Guide to End-of-Life Issues

Family Caregiver Organizer

Family Caregiver Answer Book

Instant Caregiver Kit

The

Senior's Guide
to Easy Computing
HANDBOOK

Microsoft Windows XP, Vista, Windows 7
and Apple Mac OS X

By Rebecca Sharp Colmer and Flip Colmer
EKLEKTIKA PRESS
Chelsea, Michigan

Library of Congress Card No. 2010926270
ISBN: 978-0-9823250-1-8

Printed in the United States of America

Table of Contents

Table of Contents

Table of Contents

PART 4: Windows XP Operating System

Table of Contents

Table of Contents

Table of Contents

PART 6: Windows 7 Operating System

Table of Contents

Table of Contents

Table of Contents

PART 7: Apple Mac OS X Operating System

Table of Contents

Table of Contents

PART 8: The Internet

Table of Contents

Table of Contents

Disclaimer

Every effort has been made to make this book as complete as possible and as accurate as possible. However, there may be mistakes both typographical and in content. Therefore, this text should be used as a general guide and not the ultimate source of information.

LIMIT OF LIABILITY/DISCLAIMER OF WARRANTY: THE PUBLISHER AND THE AUTHORS MAKE NO REPRESENTATIONS OR WARRANTIES WITH RESPECT TO THE ACCURACY OR COMPLETENESS OF THE CONTENTS OF THIS WORK AND SPECIFICALLY DISCLAIM ALL WARRANTIES, INCLUDING WITHOUT LIMITATION WARRANTIES OF FITNESS FOR A PARTICULAR PURPOSE. NO WARRANTY MAY BE CREATED OR EXTENDED BY SALES OR PROMOTIONAL MATERIALS. THE ADVICE AND STRATEGIES CONTAINED HEREIN MAY NOT BE SUITABLE FOR EVERY SITUATION. THIS WORK IS SOLD WITH THE UNDERSTANDING THAT THE PUBLISHER IS NOT ENGAGED IN RENDERING LEGAL, ACCOUNTING, OR OTHER PROFESSIONAL SERVICES. IF PROFESSIONAL ASSISTANCE IS REQUIRED, THE SERVICES OF A COMPETENT PROFESSIONAL PERSON SHOULD BE SOUGHT. NEITHER THE PUBLISHER NOR THE AUTHORS SHALL BE LIABLE FOR DAMAGES ARISING HEREFROM. THE FACT THAT AN ORGANIZATION OR WEB SITE IS REFERRED TO IN THIS WORK AS A CITATION AND/OR POTENTIAL SOURCE OF FURTHER INFORMATION DOES NOT MEAN THAT THE AUTHORS OR THE PUBLISHER ENDORSES THE INFORMATION THE ORGANIZATION OR WEB SITE MAY PROVIDE OR RECOMMENDATIONS IT MAY MAKE. FURTHER, READERS SHOULD BE AWARE THAT INTERNET WEB SITES LISTED IN THIS WORK MAY HAVE CHANGED OR DISAPPEARED BETWEEN WHEN IT WAS WRITTEN AND WHEN IT IS READ. NEITHER THE PUBLISHER NOR AUTHORS SHALL BE LIABLE FOR ANY LOSS OF PROFIT OR ANY OTHER COMMERCIAL DAMAGES, INCLUDING BUT NOT LIMITED TO SPECIAL, INCIDENTAL, CONSEQUENTIAL, OR OTHER DAMAGES. THE AUTHORS AND PUBLISHER SPECIFICALLY DISCLAIM ANY LIABILITY, LOSS, OR RISK, PERSONAL OR OTHERWISE, WHICH IS INCURRED AS A CONSEQUENCE, DIRECTLY OR INDIRECTLY, OF THE USE AND APPLICATION OF ANY OF THE CONTENTS OF THIS BOOK.

Getting The Most From This Book

This is a book that assumes you are a beginner or intermediate computer user.

It is best to sit down in front of a computer as you read this book. That way you can do, or see, what we are describing in the book.

Like most new skills, practice makes perfect. If you are new to computers, you will need to learn and practice these skills.

This book was written primarily for PC users. PC users should start with Parts 1, 2, and 3, then go to the part that covers your operating system: Part 4 for XP; Part 5 for Vista or Part 6 for Windows 7. Then finish with Parts 8 and 9.

We included a Mac section because we are now getting regular inquiries for Mac information. If you are a Mac user, start with Parts 1 and 2, skip Parts 3, 4, 5 and 6, and go straight to Part 7. Then finish with Parts 8 and 9.

At the end of each operating system section (Parts 4–7) there are 101 computing tips specific to that operating system. In addition, there is a mini-index just for that chapter, for easier reference. After the Internet section we've also included 25 Internet tips to help ease you onto the Information Superhighway that we call the Internet.

If you are a PC user and upgrading from a previous version of Windows, or switching from PC to Mac, or vice versa, you may need to change some habits that you have established. We hope that our collection of basic information helps you with your transition.

Objectives, Limitations, Assumptions

Let us make one thing clear right at the beginning: this book is not a textbook on how to learn everything there is to know about computers. Rather, it is an organized collection of computer, Internet, and e-mail fundamentals.

This is a crash course in "basics." It's simple. It's fun. It will get you going fast!

This book will help you to become computer functional, but not necessarily computer literate. We'll leave the techno-babble to the "propeller heads." We're going to give you some basics so you can make good use of your computer starting today!

One assumption we made as we wrote this book is that you have a broadband Internet connection. That means you connect to the Internet via a cable modem, a DSL line or a satellite dish. It also means that you can go out on the Internet by just opening your e-mail client or Web browser.

If you have a dialup connection, in other words, you use your telephone line to access the Internet, you will need to connect to the Internet first, before you accomplish any of the tasks that reference the Internet.

We Want To Hear From You!

Send us an e-mail about your computing stories. Feel free to e-mail us your questions. We'll be glad to help if we can. If you have a question, please include the following information:

- Type of computer and operating system you are using.
- Internet Service Provider and type of connection.
- What you are trying to do and which program you are using.

Go to our Web site: www.TheSeniorsGuide.com and click on **Contact Us**.

You can always contact us the old-fashioned way:

The Senior's Guide Series
EKLEKTIKA Press, Inc.
P.O. Box 157
Chelsea, MI 48118

PART 1

Computing Basics

General Computing Information
for PC and Mac Users

Computing Basics

What Is A Personal Computer?

A personal computer is a stand-alone computer that is equipped with a central processing unit (CPU), one or more disk drives, random access memory (RAM), a monitor, a keyboard, and a mouse. Or, you may have a laptop computer. They come in an assortment of colors, shapes, and sizes. Think of your computer as your personal assistant.

Is A Mac A PC?

No. PC stands for personal computer. The first personal computer was produced by IBM and was called the IBM-PC. Over time, the term PC came to mean IBM manufactured, or IBM compatible personal computers to the exclusion of other types of computers such as Apple Macintosh. And if you've seen those cute commercials on TV, you know a PC today refers to a computer that uses a Windows operating system.

Although the Apple Macintosh (Mac) is small and personal, it uses a different operating system than a PC so it is not called a PC.

Think of it as the difference between a cassette tape and audio CD. The result is the same, beautiful music playing for your enjoyment. However, CDs and tapes are not interchangeable due to the different operating systems that run them.

Why Should I Have A Computer?

Computers are electronic tools that serve many functions. They can be used for fun and business. The possibilities are unlimited. Here are just a few things you can do with a computer: manage your finances, write letters, write a book, organize caregiving records, play the stock market, trace your family history, shop from home, pay bills, meet friends in a chat room, connect with your kids and grandkids, debate popular issues, play games, listen to music, watch movies, and so much more.

Types Of Computers

There are two broad categories of computers: stay-at-home (desktop) and portable (laptops, notebooks and netbooks). These days, most home computers are small enough to sit right on your desk. Portable computers are much smaller and are easily transported. They are lightweight and can sit comfortably in your lap. They run on batteries or can connect to household electricity. Laptops can be just as powerful in their computing abilities as desktops, but they usually cost more.

Hardware

Hardware is a term for the physical components that are included when you purchase a computer. They include the system box, monitor, and mouse. You can purchase additional hardware items such as modems, CD-ROM drives, DVD drives, video and digital cameras and whatever else the "propeller heads" invent.

By itself, hardware is not capable of doing anything. Look at your stereo. It sits there looking nice, without emitting sounds until the hardware pieces are given the sounds to play. Your computer needs something to make it work. That something is software.

Software

Software tells the hardware how to work, what to do, and when to do it. Software is what gives your computer its identity. It includes the basic operating system, utility, or application programs, all expressed in a language your hardware understands.

There is software to tell your computer to do just about any task. Think about when you first balanced your checkbook. Either someone showed you how to do it or you followed the instructions on the back of your statement. Those instructions "programmed" you on how to do the task at hand: balancing your checkbook. Those instructions were your "software" and you were the "hardware" that did the work.

Applications

Software applications are programs that a computer uses so that the machine accomplishes predetermined tasks. Each application performs a specific kind of work such as word processing, desktop publishing, accounting, personal finance, etc. There is an application for just about any task you can think of. Do you want to organize your stamp collection? Do you want to organize your caregiving records? There's software to help you do just that.

A utility program is an after-market application that does housekeeping operations to assist you in maintaining and improving your computer's performance.

Operating System

An operating system is the master control program for the computer. It is the stored information that your computer needs to operate. Without an operating system all of the hardware would just sit there and collect dust. The hardware is like your skeleton, muscles, and organs. The software is like your brain. Without a brain you would just sit there and collect dust, too!

Random Access Memory (RAM)

RAM is the computer's primary working memory. RAM is used for short-term storage while the computer does its work. It is read/write memory.

RAM is distinguished from ROM, which is read-only memory. The more RAM you have the more your computer can do at one time. RAM is volatile memory. It needs to be running to "remember" what it is doing. In case of a system failure or power interruption, you will lose all of your work in RAM that you have not saved on a disk drive. Save your work frequently.

RAM vs. Hard Drive Storage

Hard Drive Storage is where programs and files are kept, RAM is where programs work. The amount of space a program needs to be stored on the hard drive has nothing to do with how much RAM is needed to run the program.

Disk Drives

Disk drives allow you to store and move data from, and to, different types of media. There are several types of drives: floppy drives, hard drives, CD-ROM drives, and DVD drives, external hard drives, removable drives and portable drives.

Because the computer world is ever changing, expect to see new drives in the future that will run our programs faster and make our tasks much simpler. In the computer world, change is good. However, you do not have to change computers every time a "new" improvement is made. The biggest differences in drives is their storage size or capacity, and how fast they find and access information.

Floppy Drive

The floppy disk drive reads data from, and writes data to, a small disk. The most common type is the 3.5" drive. While still a component of some existing computers, floppy drives are moving into obsolescence as the popularity of flash drives and other portable media drives increase. In fact, the floppy disk drive is no longer standard equipment on most new computers today.

Hard Drive

The hard drive, or hard disk, is your computer's main storage device. With a PC, it's called the C:/ drive and pronounced "see" drive. On a Mac, it is called "Macintosh HD". Data is magnetically stored there. It stores programs and data files. A typical hard disk holds 80+ gigabytes of storage.

CD-ROM Drive

CD-ROMs are compact discs, read-only, removable storage media. CD-ROMs read the data encoded on the disc and then transfer this data to the computer. The RW-CD-ROM drive is a re-writable CD-ROM drive. It allows you to read, erase, and use it repeatedly like a floppy drive.

Not all CD-ROM disks are re-writable. Some are re-writable multiple times, some only once and some not at all. Read the label!

CD-ROM discs are read using CD-ROM drives. Virtually all modern CD-ROM drives can also play audio CDs as well as video CDs and other data standards when used in conjunction with the right software.

DVD Drive

DVD stands for digital versatile disc or digital video disc. It is an optical disc storage media format. Its main uses are video and data storage. DVDs are of the same dimensions as compact discs (CDs), but store more than six times as much data.

DVD drives read DVDs. A CD-ROM drive cannot read a DVD. However, DVD drives can read CD-ROMs. And yes, there are DVD-RW drives and disks for multiple uses.

Flash Drive/Thumb Drives

A USB Flash Drive consists of a flash memory data storage device integrated with a USB (Universal Serial Bus) interface. Flash drives are typically removable and rewritable, much smaller than a floppy disk but with a greater storage capacity.

Computer Components

Monitor

Sometimes the Monitor is referred to as a CRT (cathode ray tube) and sometimes it is called a video display unit. The monitor attaches to the video output of the computer and produces a visual display. These days most computers come with a flat panel display. Some computers, such as the Apple iMac, have the monitor and system box all as one unit.

QWERTY Keyboard

It is the standard typewriter keyboard layout, used for computer keyboards. It is the most frequently used input device for all computers. The keyboard provides a set of alphabetic, numeric, punctuation, symbol, and control keys. Keep in mind that not all computers use the QWERTY keyboard.

Figure 1: QWERTY Keyboard

Mouse

The mouse is a control device. It controls the pointer on your computer screen. It is housed in a palm-sized case. The typical PC mouse includes the standard two buttons plus a wheel situated between them. Use your index finger to operate the small wheel. A Mac mouse generally has only one button, but by pressing on one side or the other, it acts like a two button mouse.

Figure 2: Cordless PC Mouse

When you move the mouse on your desk, the corresponding arrow, commonly known as the pointer, moves on the computer screen. Think of it as a remote control for your computer. Move the mouse left and right, the pointer moves left and right. Move the mouse forward and backward, the pointer moves up and down the screen. Using the mouse to command the computer to do most tasks can eliminate many keyboard strokes.

Figure 3: Mac Magic Mouse

The flashing bar, known as the cursor, is where the work will take place on the computer screen. To move the cursor with the mouse, place the pointer where you want the cursor to appear and click the mouse.

One mouse click (one click) is one quick press and release of the left button of the mouse. A right-click is one press and release of the right mouse button.

If your computer came with a corded mouse, you can purchase a wireless mouse to make your workspace less cluttered.

Using Your Mouse

To use a mouse, first place it on a flat surface or a mouse pad.

Pointing. To point to something on the screen, move the mouse across the mouse pad until the pointer is in the spot where you want it. The pointer will move in the same direction that you move the mouse.

Clicking. Single-clicking is probably the most used mouse function. To click something, point at it and quickly press and release the left mouse button. Do not hold down the button. Generally when you see "click" it refers to a left-click. A right-click is sometimes used to find a shortcut or alternate menu.

Double-clicking. Point and quickly click the mouse button in rapid succession, twice. Double-clicking is used to initiate action.

Dragging. To drag, place the mouse pointer where you want to start the drag, press and hold down the mouse button, and then Drag the mouse to the ending spot. When you have completed the drag, release the mouse button. Dragging allows you to select text, to move items, and to perform other tasks.

With a laptop, you generally do not use a mouse. A trackpad or other pointing device does the same functions as the mouse. Depending on your manufacturer, move your finger across the trackpad, and tap the trackpad as you would move and click the mouse.

Expansion Slots And USB Ports

Your system has expansion slots so you can add additional hardware known as peripherals or add-ons. Some slots may already be taken for a sound card or video card. Expansion cards give the computer additional capabilities.

USB (Universal Serial Bus) ports allow true plug and play capability. If you get a new device, such as a digital camera that is USB, in all likelihood, you will have little to do to set it up for use. Simply plug in the USB plug from the component to the computer's USB port and the computer will take care of everything else.

Multimedia

Multimedia is a term used to describe any program that incorporates some combination of sound, music, written text, pictures, animation, and video. Almost all of the computers on the market today are multimedia capable.

Printers

A printer is a device designed to print your computer-generated documents onto paper. Printers vary in their quality, speed, graphics capabilities, fonts, and even paper usage. There are dozens of brands of printers. The four most popular types of printers are dot matrix, ink jet (bubble jet), laser printers, and photo quality printers.

Most printers are inexpensive. Buy a good one.

Modems

A modem is the communications hardware that allows your computer to send and receive information from other computers, over a telephone line, cable TV line or satellite dish. Most new computers come with internal telephone modems. You will need special modems for DSL, cable or satellite communication devices, usually supplied by the provider.

You will need a modem (and a telephone line, cable line, or satellite dish) to hook up to online services and the Internet.

If you use a satellite dish, cable TV or a DSL line to connect to the Internet, the modem you will use will most likely be external.

PART 2

Getting Set-Up

How Do I Get Started?

First, you need a computer or at least access to one. You can get access to computers at libraries, schools, recreation centers, cyber-cafes and senior centers, just to name a few places.

If you are still shopping for a computer, get as much information as you can before making the purchase. Be prepared to receive contradictory opinions. Everyone has their own opinion on what is best and what to avoid. Especially on whether to buy a PC or a Mac!!

Because computer technology is changing rapidly, make sure you are not buying something that will soon be obsolete. Before making your decision, collect information and advice from friends, family and computer store personnel.

One way to test the water is to borrow some computer time from your kids and grandkids! For most new computer purchases, it is not necessary to spend thousands of dollars. In fact, your first computer should be low cost until you become a big user. If you are concerned that you may not need all of the bells and whistles being offered, get a second opinion.

Connections

Your desktop computer will come with a complete set of instructions on how to set it up. It will tell you what cables need connecting, and to where. Most manufacturers have even color-coded the connections. For example, red to red, green to green, etc. There will be a written "quickstart" guide for you to read, even though the detailed instructions about the computer are found in the computer's Help menu.

Here are the basic connections you need to make:

- Connect the video cable from the monitor to the monitor connector on the back of the computer.
- Connect the keyboard cable to the keyboard connector on the back of the computer.

- Connect the mouse cable to the mouse connector on the back of the computer or the keyboard.
- Connect the printer to the printer port on the back of the computer.
- Connect the power cord for the monitor to the back of the monitor. The other end will plug into the power source.
- Connect the power cord for the computer to the back of the PC. The other end will plug into the power source.

Adding A Printer

Adding a printer to your computer is easy. Simply connect the printer cable to your computer, and turn on the printer. The computer should recognize that a new piece of equipment has been added. If it does not, restart your computer.

After the computer has configured itself for this new printer, it will tell you it is ready to go.

Sometimes a computer can get confused and might ask you for an installation disk. All new printers come with one so you should have it ready just in case you need it. If you are asked for the installation disk, insert it into the correct drive, press Enter on your keyboard and the computer should get the information it needs from the disk.

Turning On A Desktop Computer

After you make all of the connections and plug in the power cord, turn on the power switches or buttons. Generally, both the system box and the monitor have a power button. The power button on the system box is typically located on the front of the machine. You should see an indicator light go on to let you know the machine is on. The power switch for the monitor is usually located on the front panel. There will be other adjustment buttons on your monitor to fine-tune the picture, just like on your TV.

You should always use a surge protector. They are available at most hardware, computer, department or appliance stores.

Always follow the prescribed shut-down procedures for your computer. You should not just turn it off. It is not the end of the world if you shut down improperly. You may get some extra messages cautioning you not to "do that again".

There will be times when your computer will crash or freeze-up for no apparent reason. **DON'T PANIC!** It's not your fault! It is the nature of computers to get confused every once in awhile. Just turn it off!

PART 3

Common Items For
All Versions Of Windows

Mac Users can skip to Part 7

Booting Up

Booting up is a term for starting your personal computer. It initiates an automatic routine that clears the memory, loads the operating system, and prepares the computer for use.

To start the computer:

- If this is your first start-up, make a quick check of the cables and plugs to make sure they are all connected.
- If you have a floppy-disk drive, check that drive to be sure it is empty. The computer is looking for instructions to start-up. It will take the instructions from either the floppy drive or the internal hard drive.
- If a floppy that is not a start-up disk is in the "A" drive, your PC will display a "non-system disk or disk error" message; and it will not boot up. Relax; it's not a big deal. Just push the eject button and remove the floppy and then press the spacebar on your keyboard.
- Turn on the surge protector switch (if you're using one), and turn on the computer and monitor power buttons. If you are using a laptop, open the lid and push the power button.

You will hear the machine begin to grumble and grind, and various lights may blink. You'll probably hear a beep. This is normal. At about the same time you will see some technical messages scrolling by. You do not have to read the technical messages.

The pointer on the Windows Desktop turns into an hour glass or spinning circle while it is booting up. When the pointer comes back on steady, your computer is ready for use.

Icons

An icon is a little picture that represents a program, command or a file. For instance, the My Computer icon (which represents your entire computer including drives, programs and files) looks like a small computer.

Icons that have a small white arrow in the lower left corner are Shortcuts. The arrow indicates that the icon is a shortcut that points to a program, folder, or other item. A shortcut is a quick way to open a program or file. Since the Shortcut is simply a pointer to a specific program or file, you can delete the shortcut or remove it from the Desktop without actually deleting the program or file.

Figure 1: Icon and Shortcut Icon

Pointer

The pointer is the arrow you use to choose things on screen. You control the pointer by using the mouse.

If you would like to change how the pointer looks:

- Right-click in a blank area of the Desktop.
- Select Properties or Personalize from the dialog box.
- Select Mouse Pointer. You can choose from many different styles of pointers and can control how the mouse behaves.

The Pointer Becomes an "I" Bar in a Text Document.

Figure 2: The Pointer

Figure 3: A Different Looking Pointer

Figure 4: Pointer Turns Into "I" Bar

Dragging And Dropping An Icon

To move an icon to another location, you will need to drag and drop it. To drag, put the mouse pointer over the icon and hold down the left or right mouse button. As you move the mouse across your Desktop, the pointer drags the icon across the screen. Place the pointer/icon where you want it and release the mouse button. The icon drops right where you put it.

Creating A Shortcut

As mentioned earlier, a shortcut is a quick way to gain access to a program or file. And it is easy to create shortcuts. To create a Shortcut:

- Simply find the icon of what you want to gain quick access to. Let's say, 'Your Memoirs'.
- Right-click on the Your Memoirs icon.
- Select Create Shortcut. A shortcut icon appears in the folder you have open.
- Now drag the shortcut to the Desktop and you have a quick way to launch Your Memoirs without having to go through a lot of menus.

Recycle Bin

The Recycle Bin is the little wastebasket icon in the corner of your Desktop. It works much like a real recycle bin. When you want to discard files and folders, you move them to the Recycle Bin.

Figure 5: Recycle Bin

Scroll Bars

A scroll bar is a gray rectangle with small black arrows on both ends. It is on the right side of a window for vertical scrolling and on the bottom for horizontal scrolling.

When a document is so big it cannot be completely displayed on the monitor, a scroll bar appears. You can see the entire document by moving the scroll indicator up and down the screen, or right and left.

By clicking the up/down scroll arrow one time, you will move the document one line at a time.

Clicking on a blank spot above or below the scroll indicator, you will move the document up/down one page. You can continuously scroll by depressing the mouse button steadily instead of just clicking it.

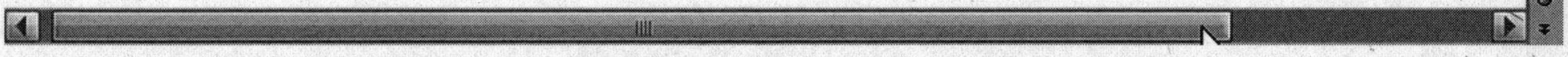

Figure 6: Horizontal and Vertical Scroll Bars

The Page Up arrow scrolls the document up and the Page Down arrow scrolls it down one full page rather than one line at a time.

Figure 7: Page Scroll Arrows

To move the document with keyboard strokes, use the Page Up and Page Down keys. These keys are generally located to the left of the number pad keys.

Dialog Boxes

A dialog box is an on-screen message box or window that enables you to choose options and send other information to a program. It conveys information to, or requests information from the user.

The computer does its best to do what you want it to. When it is asked to do something and it needs more information, it starts a dialog with you to see what your intentions are. The dialog box gives you control over how the computer does your tasks.

Sometimes the computer thinks it has enough information to do what you want and it goes its merry way. You can always initiate the dialog so that the computer will do what you want it to.

Tabs

Some dialog boxes are divided into two or more tabs (sets of options).

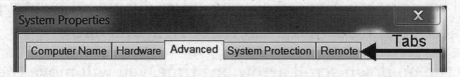

Figure 8: Tabs In A Dialog Box

Check Boxes And Radio Buttons

A check box is a small square in a dialog box. Click on as many as required. A check mark indicates that the option is active. If you click it again it will be turned off. If an option is dimmed, you cannot select it.

Figure 9: Check Box

A radio button is a small round circle. If there is a dot in the middle of it, it is active. Click the circle to activate, or deactivate the selection. Generally, only one out of a group of radio buttons can be selected.

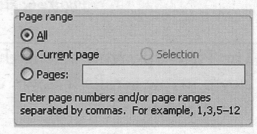

Figure 10: Radio Buttons

Command Buttons

Once you have made your selections in a dialog box, pressing the OK or Save button will save the settings selected and close the dialog box or window. Cancel will close without saving the amended settings. Apply will save the settings selected so far but will not close the dialog box, enabling you to make further changes.

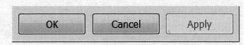

Figure 11: Command Buttons

Spin Boxes

Spin boxes let you type or select numbers. They usually have arrow buttons to allow you to increment or decrement values.

Figure 12: Spin Box

Sliding Controls

These are like sliding light switches. Some levers slide left to right; others move up and down. To adjust the level, drag and drop the sliding lever. To slide the lever: Point at the lever with the mouse and, while holding down the mouse button, move the mouse in the direction you want the sliding lever to move. As you move the mouse, the lever moves too. When you've moved the lever to the best spot, let go of the mouse button and Windows leaves the lever at its new position.

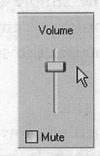

Figure 13: Slide Control

Files And Folders

A file is a collection of information, with a unique name, stored in your computer or on a removable disk. Your checking account could be one file. A single piece of correspondence could be another file. A collection of correspondence could be in one file. However, as you would in a traditional filing cabinet, a number of different letters (files) might go into a common folder (big file).

Folders allow you to organize information. Just like the file cabinet we mentioned earlier, you should organize all your files into folders. Folders can hold both files and other folders (known as subfolders). You can name folders anything you want. When you create a new folder, you get to name it. Later on, if you need to, you can rename it. And if you ever find you don't need the folder anymore, you can delete it entirely.

A window is a framed region on your screen. It is a rectangular pane with information in it. You can have a number of windows open at any one time. You can navigate from window to window simply by clicking on the border of any of the windows you want to see.

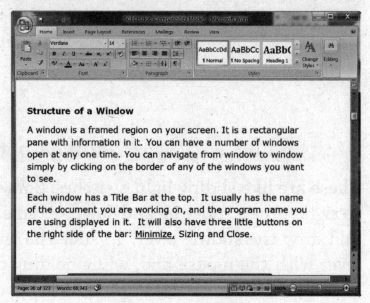

Figure 14: A Window

Each window has a Title Bar at the top. It usually has the name of the document you are working on, and the program name you are using displayed in it. It will also have three little buttons on the right side of the bar: Minimize, Sizing and Close.

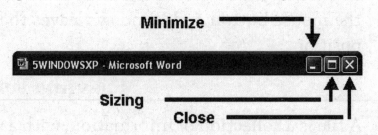

Figure 15: Title Bar

The Menu Bar is located directly under the title bar. It displays a list of command categories. In each category of commands, there are a number of choices.

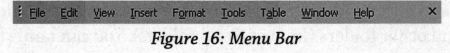

Figure 16: Menu Bar

The Program Specific Toolbar is usually located under the menu bar. It displays a row of buttons for giving commands. Each program or application will have their specific commands, but by and large, there is commonality for such things as printing, saving and use of drop down menus.

Figure 17: Program Specific Toolbar

At the bottom of the window there might be additional information. For example, in a word processing program, there might be information on pages, word count, paragraphs etc.

Figure 18: Additional Information at Bottom of Window

Menu Bars And Menus

A Menu Bar is an on-screen display that lists available categories of commands. It is usually located at the top of the program window. To choose a category or command, just click on it.

A Menu is a list of commands or options displayed on your screen, which allows you to perform a myriad of tasks. Just as you would select your choices from a restaurant menu, you select the choices of what to do on your computer.

The most frequently used menu is the Start Menu. All of your programs and files are easily accessed from here.

Each program has its menus for doing all sorts of tasks. When you click on any menu, a small box opens giving you optional commands to work with. Once you have selected an option from a menu, another box may appear. That's called opening a sub-menu. These are small windows that open and close as you use them. You are just being given more options on how to do your task at hand. If you see a little arrowhead in a menu, that means there is a sub-menu.

In our graphic below, the Menu Bar is the top line of writing. After clicking on View, a menu popped up. You can see that the Character Encoding option has a little arrowhead by it. By clicking on Character Encoding, that lead us to a sub-menu, which also has a couple of options with arrowheads on them. And the next sub-menu also has options.

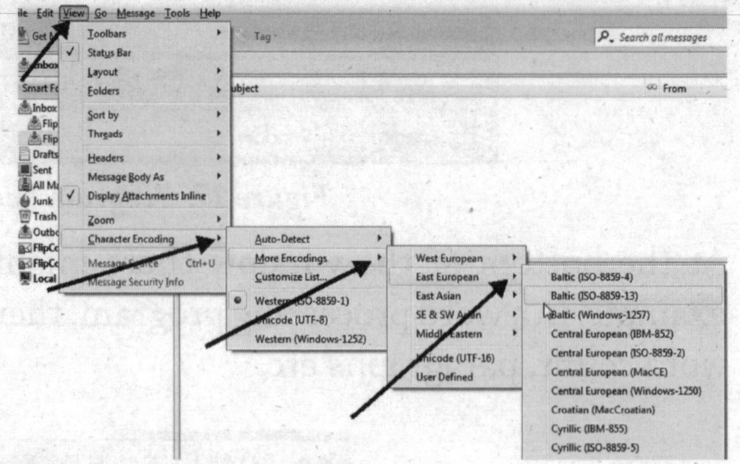

Figure 19: Menus and Sub-Menus

Basic Skills

Basic skills are used repeatedly in every program. They include selecting, cutting, pasting, copying and deleting text. You will also need to know how to open a document, save a document, and print your work.

Selecting Text

You are selecting something when you highlight it. Click at the beginning of the text you want to select. Hold down the mouse button and drag the mouse across the text that you want to work with. This may be a word, phrase, sentence, paragraph, page or even an entire document. Release the mouse button and the text between where you clicked and released will be highlighted and selected.

Cutting, Copying And Pasting

These commands are found under the Edit menu. The Cut command allows you to remove text from your document and use it elsewhere. The Copy command lets you duplicate a section of your document without removing it from the original spot. After you have cut or copied your selection, you are ready to paste. Move the cursor to the place in the document where you want the section to appear. Then select the Paste option.

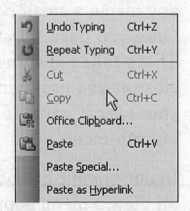

Figure 20: Edit Menu

You also have access to these commands with the Alternate Menu. The Alternate Menu is opened by right-clicking the mouse where you want to do the work.

To cut or copy, and paste with the Alternate Menu:

- Select the item to cut or copy: a few words, a file, a Web address, or any other item.
- Right-click on your selection and choose Cut or Copy from the menu depending on your needs. (Use Cut when you want to remove something. Use Copy when you want to create an exact copy of something.) Keyboard shortcut: hold down Ctrl and press X to cut or C to copy.
- Move the cursor to where you want to paste the selection, right-click on the item's destination and choose Paste. Keyboard shortcut: hold down Ctrl and press V to paste.

You can even paste information outside of the program you are working with. After you cut or copy information, it automatically goes to Windows' Clipboard. You can paste it nearly anyplace else from there.

- Open the destination window and move the mouse to the spot where you want the stuff to appear.
- Right-click the mouse and choose Paste from the pop-up menu. The item you just cut or copied immediately appears in the new place.

Undo

To undo what you've just done: Hold down the Ctrl key and press the Z key. The last keystroke you made is reversed. Or, you can click the Edit menu and then click Undo from the drop-down menu. The last command you made is undone. You can work backwards through your work as many times as you care to.

Deleting Text

Select (highlight) the text you want to delete. Press the Delete key. This is different from Cut, as this text is not stored in the computer's memory for your use. It does not go to the clipboard.

Saving A Document

One of the most important precautions you can take while working is to save your work frequently. Saving means to send the work you've just created to a disk or hard drive for safekeeping. You must specifically tell the computer to save your work.

On the File menu of the program you are working in, click Save. The save window appears. In the File Name text box there is a blinking cursor or high-lighted text. Type in the name you want the file to be called. If an acceptable name is already there, you don't have to change it. Click on Save. As you continue working on the same document, you need only to choose the Save command from the File menu. There generally is an icon of a disk on the toolbar which is also a save command.

The Save As command lets you save your work with a different name or to a different location. For example, you may change a few sentences in your original document, but you don't want to lose the original words. Preserve both versions by selecting Save As, and giving the document a new name. When you are saving something for the first time, the Save and Save As commands are identical.

Printing Your Work

To print your work:

- From the File menu, choose Print.
- After making sure all of the options are set the way you want them, click OK.

There is generally a Quick Print icon on the Program Menu Bar. It looks like a little printer. This will start the printing process without going to the File menu and the printer options dialog box.

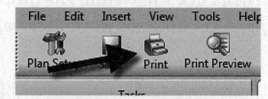

Figure 21: Quick Print Icon

Print Preview

Print Preview is an easy way to view your document before it is printed.

- Click on Print Preview and your document is shown as it will appear in print.
- If you do not like something about the print job, you can go back and adjust the document before printing.

Want to check on how that special character you picked will look? Use the zoom bar and take a look. Do the margins look okay on all the pages? This is how you can check before it goes to print.

Figure 22: Zoom Bar

Printer Configuration

You can set up default settings for your printer so that it prints the same way every time. You can still make changes for each document that you create, but it will be from these default settings.

To change these settings:

- Click on Start.
- Click Control Panel.
- Click Printers.
- Right-click on your printer.
- Select Printer Preferences. Make your adjustments here.

You can also exercise some control via the Properties option after you right-click on your printer. Mostly, you would use this to share a printer on a network.

Opening A Window

To open a window displaying the contents of a disk or folder, double-click on the icon. The window is displayed on the Desktop.

To open a window displaying a program, start the program by double clicking its icon. The program is started and displayed in a program window.

If you are working in a program, you can have two windows open: the program window and the document window. Each window has its own set of controls. Confusing? Don't worry. With a little practice, you'll be a pro at this.

Minimizing A Window

While working in an open window, you might want to temporarily hide it to work on something else. You can send the window to the Taskbar by either clicking the Minimize button in the upper right hand corner of the window, or clicking its Taskbar button on the Taskbar. The Minimize button is the square with a dash in it representing a smaller window size.

To restore the window to the Desktop, simply click on its Taskbar button and it will come back to the Desktop.

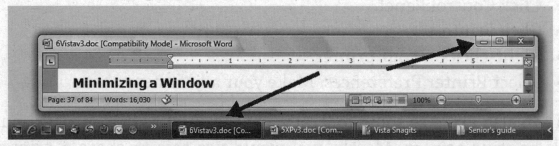

Figure 23: Minimizing a Window

Closing A Window

Running programs that you are not working in takes up computer memory resources. When you are finished working with a document or program, save your work and then close the file and/or program. To close a window, click the Close Button in the upper right hand corner of the window. It is a white X in a red square. You can also close the program by clicking on File in the upper tool bar, and then Exit. You may sometimes see the word Close, instead of Exit in the menu. In our example to the right, there is no File menu. In this case, Exit is under the Game menu.

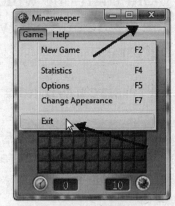

Figure 24: Closing a Program or Window

Re-sizing A Window

The button between the Minimize button and the Close button in the upper right hand corner of a window is a Sizing Button. You can click it and a full screen presentation will get smaller, but not minimize to the Taskbar. You can see that when you are in full screen, the button has two little windows displayed.

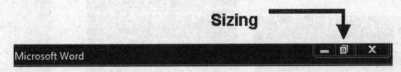

Figure 25: Sizing Button When Window is Full Screen

When you are in a little window, a single full size icon is in the button.

Figure 26: Sizing Button When Window is Less Than Full Screen

You can change the size of a window to make it easier to read, or to have more than one window open side by side on the Desktop. Rather than use the sizing buttons, you will manually control how big, or small your window becomes.

To re-size a window:

- Put the pointer on any of the window's borders. The pointer turns into a two-headed arrow.
- Drag the border to change the size of the window. The window will only get bigger or smaller in the direction of the drag. (If the pointer does not change to the double-headed arrow, make sure you are not in full screen mode. Click the upper right re-size button and then try finding the two-headed arrow.)
- To have the window change its proportions in height and width at the same time, put the pointer on any of the corners of the window. The mouse pointer again turns into a two-headed arrow.

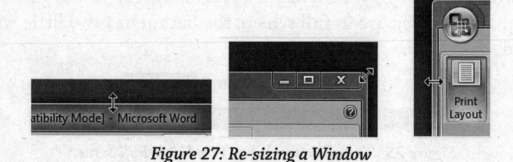

Figure 27: Re-sizing a Window

- Drag diagonally and the window reduces, or gets bigger, in size both vertically and horizontally.

Working With Programs

Program (or Application) is synonymous with software. It is a set of instructions, written in a programming language that a computer can execute, to perform your tasks in a certain way.

Accessory Programs

Accessory programs are located in the Accessories folder in the All Program menu. They include: Accessibility, Communications, Entertainment, Games, System Tools, Calculator, Imaging, Keyboard Manager, Notepad, Paint and WordPad.

Pre-loaded Software

Your computer may come with pre-loaded software that may include a word processing program, financial management tools or a digital photo program. You can find all of these programs through the All Programs menu.

Control Panel Programs

The control panel allows you to adjust how all of the pieces/parts of your computer work. You will find these programs by clicking the Start button and then selecting Control Panel.

MS-DOS Prompt

MS-DOS refers to typed code used to make the computer do its work. Windows uses a graphical representation of the MS-DOS code, which is a great improvement in user friendliness. Do not worry about this function. It is rarely used these days. Although many books still give you instructions on MS-DOS, we will not refer to it anymore in this book. If you get advanced enough to use MS-DOS so that you can look "under the hood," an in-depth MS-DOS book will be better for you.

The more you work with your computer, the more you can do with it. Eventually, you will probably think to yourself, "I'll bet there is a specialized program to help me do this task." You bet there is! You can find programs that will do just about anything.

However, before you buy a new program, make sure that you can run that program on your system. Check the system requirements (usually printed on the side of the software box). These include type of microprocessor, amount of memory, hard disk space, video card, and any other required equipment.

Today, most software ships on CD or DVD discs. You must have the appropriate drive for the particular media you buy.

You will need to install the new software onto your system. Most software applications include instructions for installing the software. I have included some basic steps for installing new software in Windows. If the instructions included with the software differ greatly from these, I recommend you use the instructions included with the software.

Software can also be purchased and downloaded via the Internet. No need to go to the store! Simply follow the instructions from the vendor's website.

Warning! Make sure you know who you are downloading from before you purchase a program.

To add a program:

- Insert the installation disc in the drive. (If you are installing from a disk that has an Auto Run feature, when you insert the disk, the installation program starts automatically.)

If the installation prompt does not come up automatically:

- Click the Start button.
- Select Run (or type Run in the Search Box and select from Program list).
- Type in the drive letter the disk is in.
- Click OK.

- Double-click the installation icon which looks like a CD and a box.
- Follow the on-screen instructions.

Once again, if the installation instructions on the box differ from what you just read, follow the manufacturer's recommendations.

Opening A Program

To start a program, find its legend in the Start menu, or its icon (or its shortcut icon) and double-click it. The program will start up. You can also start the program by opening a file that was created with it. For example, I can open Microsoft Word by clicking its Start menu legend, its icon in my programs file or its shortcut icon on my Desktop. Microsoft Word also opens when I click on the icon for this manuscript you are reading since it was created with Microsoft Word

Opening A File

You open a file the same way you open a program: find its legend through the Start menu, or its icon (or its shortcut icon) and double-click it. Not only does the file open, but the program that it was created with opens as well.

Function Keys

F1–F12: On your keyboard, there are a number of keys with special functions. Laptop keyboards are slightly different than desktop keyboards, but all the functions should still be there.

These programmable keys are called function keys. They provide special functions depending on the software you are using. Check your software's documentation for the specific functions of each key. (Remember, not all keyboards are the same.)

Esc: The escape key cancels a command or an operation. It is located in the upper left hand corner of the keyboard.

Numeric Keypad: A calculator-style set of keys for entering numbers. The keypad is located on the right side of the keyboard.

NumLock: The Number Lock key switches the right-hand keypad on a full sized keyboard between typing numbers and being used as cursor keys. This key is located in the upper left corner of the numeric key pad.

Arrow Keys: The keys that move the cursor on screen. The arrow keys move the cursor in the direction indicated by the arrow on each key: one character left or right or one line up or down. They are located to the right of the right hand shift key.

Page Up (PgUp) and **Page Down** (PgDn) keys: These keys move the cursor to the preceding screen (PgUp) or the next screen (PgDn).

Ctrl: The control key pressed in combination with other keys, acts as a short-cut to execute commands and select commands from the drop down menus.

Delete (Del): This key deletes the character to the left of the cursor. It acts just like the back space key on a typewriter.

Word Processing Overview

A word processor is a program that enables you to create documents that you might have once created with a typewriter. You can create letters, memos, reports, lists, invitations, and much, much more. To make the job easier, most word processors offer grammar and spell checking tools. Some include built-in reference works such as synonym finders and almanacs. The most popular word processors are Microsoft Word and WordPerfect.

Spreadsheet Overview

A spreadsheet program lets you create electronic ledgers in which calculations are done instantly and automatically. Spreadsheet programs can translate your data into charts and graphs. The most popular spreadsheet programs are Microsoft Excel and Lotus 1-2-3.

Games

There are many games available for your PC. If there is a game you have been playing for years, chances are it has been created in an electronic format. Chess, bridge, solitaire, and more games exist for your entertainment. Windows comes with a few games. They are located in the Accessories, Games directory. You can always buy more.

Multitasking

Multitasking means that your computer can execute more than one program at a time. You can have more than one window open at a time. For example, you are able to write using your word processing program while your spreadsheet program prints a report.

Antivirus, Malware, Spyware

Every computer user should practice safe computing. It is important enough that we will address this again in the operating system sections. There are a number of threats to your computer in the form of malicious software that can take control of your computer, steal data from you or even crash your computer. To practice safe computing, every computer user should use software designed to combat these problems. You should always use some form of the following programs on your computer:

Figure 28: An Arsenal of Anti-Malware Programs

- Anti-virus such as Avira Antivir, AVG Free, Symantec Norton Anti-Virus or McAfee Anti-Virus
- Anti-Spyware such as Spybot and SpyWareBlaster
- Anti-Malware such as AdAware

These are just a few of the many programs out there to help keep your computer safe. Some are free and some require subscription payments. Regardless of how much, or how little you spend on protection, you need to protect your computer.

PART 4

Windows XP
Operating System

Windows XP Operating System

Windows XP is an older operating system that lets you give orders to your computer. The system acts on your commands. Microsoft launched Windows XP in 2001. Since then, they have released several service packs or patches to help your computer run more smoothly.

Microsoft does not let its service packs install on illegitimate copies of Windows XP. If the service pack gives you a weird message about "Activation," contact the person who sold or gave you Windows XP. There are different versions of Windows XP for business and home use. Most home users do not need a business version of Windows XP.

To identify your operating system and service pack version, right-click on the My Computer icon, select Properties and then the General Tab.

What Should I See On The Screen During Start-Up?

With Windows XP, the first screen you will see before the Desktop is a "user" choice screen. Windows XP allows several people to work on the same computer, yet it keeps everybody's work separate. You can set-up your computer with different settings, themes, choices and passwords, for each user in your household. If you do this, then at start-up, the computer will ask you to click on your user name.

After the start-up, what you should see on the monitor is the Windows Desktop. It is the home base like the physical desk where your computer sits. Several tools to get you started are placed on the background area. These include a Taskbar, icons, and a Start button.

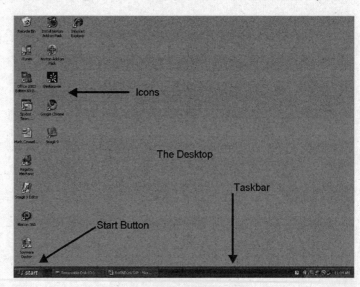

Figure 32: The Desktop

There will be variations from computer to computer on what the Desktop looks like. You will be able to customize the look of your Desktop to suit your artistic feelings.

Basic Controls And Mechanics

Desktop

When you start your computer, you will see several screens go by before you arrive at the main Windows screen, which is the Desktop.

The Desktop is the working area (background) of the Windows display on your computer. Look at your desk at home or work. It is the area where you do your paperwork. You pull a file, letter, or your checkbook from a drawer, do some work, and put it back when you are finished. The Desktop of the computer (on the monitor screen) is where you will pull out your electronic files, write electronic letters or work in your computer-based checkbook. The Desktop has three main parts: Taskbar, Start menu, and Recycle Bin.

Taskbar

Figure 33: Taskbar

The Taskbar is the horizontal bar that normally lives along the bottom of the Desktop (although you can move it to any edge by dragging it from edge to edge. If it doesn't move, right-click on the Taskbar and click Lock the Taskbar to remove the check mark by its name).

On the Taskbar, the Start button is on the left. Displayed in small rectangles near the middle of the Taskbar are the programs that are running. Near the right side, you will see the programs or tasks that start automatically when you start Windows. On the far right, you will see the time displayed. The Taskbar allows you to start your navigation process through all of the computer files.

Figure 34: Taskbar Buttons

Taskbar buttons appear to the right of the Start button, near the middle of the Taskbar, to identify any open applications or programs currently being used. If a program is minimized (meaning it does not appear on the screen, but is still being used), clicking on it from the Taskbar brings it back on-screen. You can easily switch to a different window by clicking its Taskbar button.

The Start button And Start Menu

The Start button is the tool that takes you almost anywhere in Windows. It is located on the Taskbar. Clicking on the Start button brings up a single menu from which many menus and programs can be accessed.

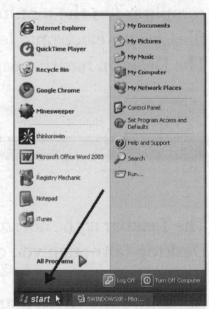

To display the Start menu, click the Start button. Your Start menu will change as you add more programs to your computer. That's why your Start menu and mine will not look the same.

The left side of the Start Menu is where you will see your most frequently used programs. To put a program on your Start button drag any icon from your Desktop onto the Start button.

Figure 35: Start button and Start Menu

Pinning To The Start Menu

You will notice that on the Start Menu, on the left side, there is a top and bottom section. The top section is fixed. Those programs are pinned to the Start Menu and do not leave. The bottom section is for recently used programs. These will change based on your usage.

However, if you would like to keep some of those programs in the upper "always there" section, you can pin them there. To pin a program to the Start Menu:

- Right-click on the program icon.
- Select Pin To Start Menu. The program icon will shift to the upper section.

To unpin a selection:

- Right-click on a program icon in the pinned area.
- Select Unpin From Start Menu. The icon will leave the upper section.

Shutting Down Your Computer

It is important to use the correct shutdown procedure. You should never *just* turn off your computer.

Before you shut down, always save the files you are working on. Always close any open windows before shutting down your computer. This will help to protect your files from data corruption.

To shut down:

- Click the Start button and select Shut Down or Turn Off Computer.
- Select the Shut Down option.
- Click the OK or Yes.

You will see a screen that tells you it is safe to turn off your PC. Turn off the power to your computer. Do not forget to turn off the monitor, too.

If you are using a laptop, you generally shut down the same way. However, most laptops will go to sleep if you just close the lid. So if you are intending to shut the laptop down, use the normal shutdown method.

Frozen Computer

Your computer may experience a puzzling failure from time to time. Sometimes it may just freeze up, for no reason at all. **DO NOT WORRY. YOU DID NOT DO IT!** It is just the nature of computers to get confused on occasion. When this happens, your mouse may not respond to clicks and the keyboard may stop working. The darn machine does not respond. You may have to restart your computer.

First, try to shutdown the frozen program. Press these three keys at the same time: Ctrl, Alt, Del and follow the prompts. Find the program that is not responding, select it, and click End Program. If the computer responds, you are back in business.

If that didn't work, try the menu method. Click the Start button and select Shut Down/Turn Off Computer. Select the Restart Computer button. Click the Yes button.

If that didn't work, try the alternate method. Press these two keys at the same time, Ctrl and Alt. While holding them down, press DEL three times.

Third, the last ditch method, turn off the power switch. On some computers, you have to hold the power button in until it actually shuts down. When you restart the computer, you will probably get a message telling you to shut down properly next time. You can ignore this message as you were trying to unfreeze your computer.

Re-sizing A Window

You may want to change the size of the window to make it easier to read. There are several ways to re-size a window.

- Put the pointer on any of the window's borders. The mouse pointer turns into a two-headed arrow. Drag the border to change the size of the window. (Does not work if window is in full screen mode.)

Figure 36: Double Headed Arrow for Re-sizing

- Use the Minimize and Maximize buttons that are located in the upper right corner of every window. If you click on the Minimize button, the box with a dash in it, the window disappears. However, you will notice the program button is still on the Taskbar. Instead of quitting the program entirely, minimizing closes only the window of the program. To maximize or open the window again, click on its button on the Taskbar.
- If the next box over from the Minimize button has a single square in it, clicking it will enlarge the working window to the size of your monitor screen. If there are two boxes in the little square, clicking it will reduce the size from full screen.

Figure 37: Window Sizing Buttons

- Clicking the last square, the one with the "X" in it, actually exits or quits the program.

Moving A Window

You may want to rearrange where a window is located. Follow these steps to move a window:

- Place the pointer on the window's title bar.
- Drag the title bar to the location you want and release the mouse button.

Figure 38: Grabbing and Moving a Window

You cannot move a window that is full screen. You must re-size it to something other than full or minimized to rearrange your windows.

Closing A Window

Always remember to close the program when you are finished working in it. Otherwise, it will be taking up memory that other programs may need.

To close a program:

- Save your work.
- Click the Close (X) button in the title bar of the window of the program.

- If you have not saved your work, the program asks you if you want to. Click Yes to save it, click No to lose it.
- The program window disappears.

Alternate method if the close button does not work:

- Click on File in the menu bar.
- Save your work.
- Click Close from the same drop down menu.

Using Menus And Sub-Menus

It is as simple as this:

- On the menu bar, choose the category of the command that you want. The menu opens.
- Click on the command you want.
- If a sub-menu opens, it is just giving you more options of how to accomplish your task at hand.

Shortcut Menus

A shortcut menu, or alternate menu, is a hidden menu that can be opened at any time. Almost every object on your Desktop has one. If you right-click on the item, the shortcut menu will appear.

Windows XP Tasks

Exploring Drives

The (A:) drive is the floppy drive. Older computers used to have two floppy drives, and the second one was the (B:) drive. Your computer may not have an (A:) or (B:) drive.

The (C:) drive is the hard disk drive. This drive is non-removable. The (D:) drive is usually the CD-ROM drive. Sometimes it is the (E:) drive. You can see all of your drives by clicking on the My Computer icon.

As more drives are added, they are assigned a letter by the computer. Be careful of how many drives you have hooked up at any one time. Too many drives connected (such as a camera card reader, iPod cradle, external hard drive, etc.) at the same time can bog down your machine. If it's USB, and you're not using it, unplug it.

Finding A File Or Folder

When you are looking for a particular file or folder, and you are not sure where it is located on your computer, you can use the Find (Search) command instead of opening numerous folders. The Find command lets you quickly search a specific drive or your entire computer. To find a file or folder:

- Click the Start button, point to Find/Search, and then click Files or Folders. The Find dialog box appears.
- In Named, type the file or folder name you want to find.
- Click the Look In down arrow, or click Browse to specify where to search, generally the C: drive.
- Click Find Now. The results of the search will appear.

A word to the wise: start filing your information in an orderly manner at the beginning of your computer experience. It will make life easier.

Opening A File Or Folder

To find and open a file or folder:

- On the Desktop, double-click My Computer.
- Double-click the drive that contains the file or folder you want to open.
- Double-click on each folder in your filing structure until you find the file or folder you are looking for.
- Double-click the file or folder.

If you have recently opened a file that you want to look at again, check My Documents. You can also open files and folders from the File Open command in the application.

Naming A File Or Folder

If you're saving something for the first time, Windows XP asks you to name the file or document. Type something descriptive. Use only letters, numbers, and spaces between the words. You can't use any of the following characters: : / \ * | < > ? "

The last three letters (suffix) of a file name designate an extension. An extension identifies the format of the file. It is preceded by a period. Every file is in a specific format. There are many different formats. By naming a file with an extension, you tell the computer which format the file is in. That way the computer knows what format to use each time you want to work with that file. Most programs automatically add the extension suffix when you save your work. For example, Microsoft Word documents end with the file extension .doc while Microsoft Excel spreadsheets end with the extension .xls.

Renaming A File Or Folder

It is simple to rename a file or folder. To rename:

- Select the file or folder you want to rename.
- On the File menu, click Rename.
- Type a name and press Enter.

Alternatively:

- Select the file or folder you want to rename.
- Right-click on it and select Rename from the shortcut menu.
- Type a name and press Enter.

Warning! Renaming program and system files is not recommended!

Copying And Moving A File Or Folder

When you create files and folders, you may want to copy or move them to another location. For example, the tax return you just finished is in its own folder named Taxes 2015. You would really like the Taxes 2015 folder to be in the Finances 2015 folder, so you move it to Finances 2015.

To copy or move a file or folder:

- Select the file or folder you want to copy or move. You can select multiple items. To select nonadjacent items, hold down the Ctrl key and click the items you want to select. To select adjacent items, hold down the SHIFT key, select the first item you want to work with, then click on the last item in a row you want. All of the files between the two will become selected. To select all of the items in a window, on the Edit menu, click Select All.
- On the Edit menu, click Copy (to copy the file) or Cut (to remove the file).
- Double-click the folder in which you want to place the file or folder. On the Edit menu, click Paste. The file appears in a new location.
- You can also just drag the selected icons from one folder to another if you are working with directories.

Creating A File Or Folder

To create a folder:

- On the Desktop, double-click My Computer.
- Double-click the disk drive or folder in which you want to create a folder. The drive or folder opens.
- On the File menu, point to New, and then click Folder. An alternate way is to right-click a blank area in the window. Click Folder and it will appear.
- Type a folder name, and then press Enter. The new folder appears in the location you selected.

Deleting A File And Folder

Whenever you delete a file, it is temporarily moved to the Recycle Bin on the Desktop. If you change your mind, you can restore the file. However, when you empty the Recycle Bin, all of its items are permanently deleted from your computer. To delete a file:

- Select the file(s) you want to delete, using either My Computer or Windows Explorer.
- Right-click the selected file(s) and then select the Delete command. Click Yes when prompted to confirm the deletion.

It is not a good idea to delete program files. If you want to get rid of a program, uninstall it through the Control Panel and the Add/Remove icon.

Using The Recycle Bin

The Recycle Bin is the little wastebasket icon in the corner of your Desktop and works much like a real recycle bin. To put a file or folder in the Recycle Bin:

- Right-click on the file you want to dispose of and choose Delete from the menu.
- Windows XP will ask you if you're sure you want to delete the item. Click Yes and Windows XP puts it in the Recycle Bin.

To retrieve something from the Recycle Bin, double-click the Recycle Bin icon to see your deleted items. Right-click the item you want and choose Restore.

To delete something permanently, just delete it from inside the Recycle Bin. To delete everything in the Recycle Bin: right-click on the Recycle Bin and choose Empty Recycle Bin.

File Management

File management is just that, managing or organizing your directories and files to make your computer as efficient as possible. Much like a filing cabinet has file folders, a hard disk can be divided into folders. A folder can contain files and/or other folders. You can store like files together in a folder.

Customizing Your Desktop

If you don't like the standard color scheme on your Desktop, you can change it. You can use predefined color schemes or make up your own. If your color selections are too wild they may cause eye strain!

To select a background or pattern for the Desktop:

- Right-click on the Desktop.
- Select Properties. The Display Properties dialog box appears. Select Desktop.
- Select Background. Make your changes. Then click Apply and Okay to close the dialog box.

To change any of the screen elements:

- Right-click on the Desktop. Select Properties.
- Click on the Appearance tab. Display the Scheme drop-down menu and select the color scheme that tickles your fancy.
- Click Apply and Okay to close the dialog box.

Playing A CD

Playing music with the CD Player is very simple. A feature called auto-play detects when you insert a CD into the CD-ROM drive and automatically starts the music for you. If auto-play does not work, here is how to do it manually:

- Click the Start button.
- Select All Programs.
- Select Accessories.
- Select Entertainment.
- Select Windows Media Player.
- Insert a disk into the CD drive.
- Click Play.

Playing Media Clips And Movies

To play a media file (AVI, WAV, MID or RMI):

- Click the Start button.
- Select Programs.
- Select Accessories.
- Select Entertainment.
- Select Media Player. Windows will display the Media Player program.

- Open the File menu.
- Select Open.
- When you see the file you want to play, double-click it. To play the clip, click the Play button.

Screen Saver

A screen saver is a program that displays an image or animation on your screen when your PC is idle. It was invented to ensure that all parts of the monitor screen received equal amounts of illumination so a ghost image would not be "burned" onto the screen. Today's monitors don't have burn-in problems.

Screen savers are fun and often entertaining. You can use any number of pre-installed screen savers or you can use screen savers downloaded from the internet. You can even use any of your saved digital photos.

Windows comes with a number of screen savers. There are many more screen savers available commercially. To find the screen savers included with Windows:

- Right-click on a blank spot on the Desktop, and choose Properties to open the Display Properties dialog box.
- On the Screen Saver tab, select an option from the drop-down list.
- Click OK to make this your screen saver.

To use images you have stored on your computer as your screen saver:

- Right-click on Desktop.
- Select Screen Saver tab.
- Highlight My Pictures slide show.
- Click Apply and OK to close the dialog box.

Adding A New Program

To add a program:

- Insert the installation disk in the drive. If you are installing from a disk that has an AutoRun feature, when you insert the disk, the installation program starts automatically. If any dialog boxes open, answer the questions they ask you and click OK.

If the installation prompt doesn't come up automatically:

- Click the Start button, select Settings, and select Control Panel.
- Double-click Add/Remove programs.
- Click Install button.
- Click the Finish button. Follow the on-screen instructions.

You can also use the Run Command to install a program. To use the Run Command:

- Insert the program disk into the drive. Click the Start button.
- Select Run. The Run dialog box appears.
- Type the drive letter (ex. D:\).
- Click the OK button.
- Click the Installer (disc) icon.

Follow the on-screen instructions for installing the program.

If you have downloaded a program from the internet, find the icon for it on your Desktop and click it. A dialog box will open and guide you through the process.

Removing A Program

The best way to uninstall a program is by using the Add/Remove Program icon, located in the Control Panel.

It is not a good idea to simply delete the program folder. The original program installation may have put files in other folders and changed some of the system settings.

To remove a program:

- Click the Start button.
- Select Control Panel. You see the program icons in the Control Panel.
- Double-click the Add/Remove icon.

- Select the program you want to uninstall.
- Click the Add/Remove button.

Starting A Program

Most of the programs installed on your computer are available from the All Programs section of the Start menu.

To start a program:

- Click the Start button.
- Click All Programs. The Program menu appears.
- Click on the program name that contains the program you want to start.

If the program is stored in a folder, point to the folder. Continue until you see the program icon. Then click the icon to start the program.

Closing A Program And Saving Your Work

Always remember to close a program when you are finished working in it. Otherwise, it will be taking up memory that other programs may need.

To close a program:

- Save your work.
- Click the Close (X) button in the title bar of the window of the program.
- If you have not saved your work, the program asks you if you want to. Click Yes to save it, click No to lose it.
- The program window disappears.

Alternate method:

- Go to File.
- Save your work.
- Click Close from the same drop down menu.

Quitting A Program

To quit a program:

- Save your work before you quit a program.

- Click the Close (X) button in the upper-right corner of the program window.
- Or from the File menu, click Close.

My Computer Directory

The My Computer icon represents one way to see everything on your system. It allows you to browse drives, directories (folders), and files in separate ways. An icon that looks like a folder represents each directory.

To use My Computer to view the hard disk:

- On the Desktop, double-click My Computer. The My Computer window appears.
- Double-click the icon that represents your hard disk. Your hard disk window and its contents appear.

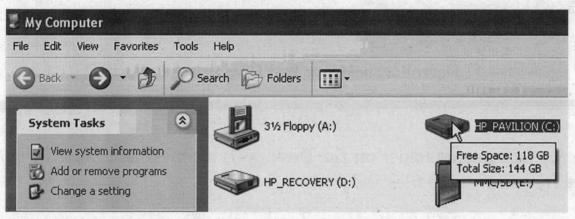

Figure 39: Looking at Your Hard Drive

Windows Explorer

Another way to see everything in your system is with Windows Explorer. Instead of opening drives and folders in separate windows, you can browse through them in a single window, in a hierarchical structure.

The left side of the Windows Explorer window contains a list of your drives and folders, and the right side displays the contents of the selected folder. You can use View menu to change how the icons in the right half of the window appear.

To use Windows Explorer to view the hard disk:

- Click the Start button.
- Select All Programs.
- Click on Accessories.
- Click on Windows Explorer.
- In the left pane, click the letter that represents your hard disk. The contents of your hard disk appear in the right pane.

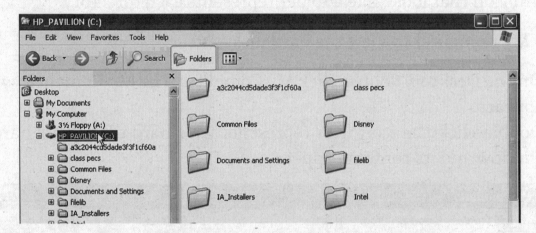

Figure 40: Looking at Your Hard Drive's Folders

My Documents

The My Documents folder on the Desktop is a convenient place for you to store frequently used files and folders.

For easy access to a file that you use frequently, you can also create a shortcut to it. A shortcut does not change the location of the file. The shortcut is just a pointer that lets you open the file quickly.

To open recently used documents click on the Start button, and then point to My Documents. A list of your documents appears. Click on a document in the list and the document opens. To move a file to the My Documents folder, drag the file to the My Documents folder on your Desktop.

To create a shortcut to a file, use the right mouse button to drag the file to the Desktop. On the menu that appears, click Create Shortcut(s). The shortcut appears on the Desktop. You can copy or move the shortcut to another location.

Good Housekeeping

Backing Up

It is very important to periodically backup all of the data files on your computer. If something happens to your computer you can always reinstall them from a copy. The copy should be made to an external hard drive, or to disks stored away from your computer. You can even back up to an online backup company such as Carbonite (www.carbonite.com).

If something happens to your data, and you do not have a backup copy, you are in a pickle. How often you backup depends on how important the data is to you.

Be sure to put your backup copies in a safe place away from your computer. In case of a disaster, you will want your backup copies in a secure location.

Hard Disk Maintenance

Over time, hard drives slow down, due to storing files in separate clusters. This is normal. To keep your system running in tip top condition, you should regularly give your hard drive a tune-up.

By using Scan Disk/Error Checking and Defragment, you will keep your computer running efficiently.

Computers store information in clusters. However, the clusters of one file may not all be stored in the same area of the hard drive. When this happens, the disk is "fragmented". The computer has to go to several places in the storage space to get it and reassemble it for you. To improve the performance, you can straighten up the disk and put files back in order.

To defragment your hard drive:

- Backup your system before you start defragmenting.
- Double-click the My Computer icon.
- Right-click the disk you want to check.
- Select Properties.

- Click the Tools tab.
- Click Defragment Now.
- Click the Start button. Windows displays the progress on screen.
- When the defragmentation is complete and you are prompted to defragment another drive, click the No button.

Scan Disk/Error Checking checks for and fixes damage to the drive. To run Scan Disk/Error Checking:

- Double-click the My Computer icon.
- Right-click the disk you want to check.
- Select Properties.
- Click the Tools tab.
- Click the Check Now button. Windows displays two Check Disk options. Check both boxes.
- Click the Start button. Windows checks your drive and if it finds any errors, it will display a dialog that explains the error and your options.
- Select a correction method. Click OK.
- Review this info and then click Close.
- If Windows wants to do the work the next time you restart your computer, say Yes.

101 Hot Computer Tips And Tricks

1. Check out The Senior's Guide website on a frequent basis, www.TheSeniorsGuide.com.

2. Consider moving up to DSL, cable or satellite if you have a dialup modem.

3. Pressing F1 opens Help information in most programs.

4. Press Ctrl, Alt, Del simultaneously to send Windows a signal to shut down. You can use this combination to quit a program that is freezing up.

5. You can select a group of files by selecting the first one and then holding down the Ctrl key while you select the others.

6. A good way to practice using the mouse is to play Solitaire. You will get the feel of the mouse by clicking and dragging.

7. If you are formatting an existing disk, be sure the disk does not contain any information that you need. Formatting erases all of the information on the disk.

8. To avoid problems, close all open programs before starting any program installation.

9. To rename a shortcut icon, simply right-click the icon, select Rename, and type in a new name. Press Enter.

10. Perform regular housekeeping and delete those files that are no longer needed.

11. A "local" access number may still be a toll call. Check with your operator to be sure that it is a local call.

12. If you subscribe to an online mailing list, be sure you know how to un-subscribe.

13. Macintosh and PC users can send e-mail to each other.

14. Always spell check your documents. Spell checkers will catch spelling errors, duplication errors, and most typical non-spelling errors.

15. When you buy software, be sure to send in the registration card. The company will then keep you posted about upgrades and future releases.

16. When describing a CD, the term "disc" is used instead of "disk". They are pronounced the same.

17. A zip drive is a type of disk with a higher density than a floppy disk. You can store more information on it than on a floppy disk.

18. If you want to see Calculator's scientific side, click View at the top of the Calculator window, and then click Scientific. To turn it back to the original, click View again and then click Standard.

19. Reshaping or re-sizing a window is an easy way to get rid of scroll bars. Just keep stretching the window until the scroll bar you do not want, goes away. No matter how hard you try, some windows cannot let you see all of the contents at one time.

20. Using keyboard shortcuts, instead of the mouse and drop-down menus, can make your work go faster.

21. The keyboard shortcut for Display Properties Box is Alt-Enter.

22. The keyboard shortcut for Bold is Ctrl-B.

23. The keyboard shortcut for Italics is Ctrl-I.

24. The keyboard shortcut for Underline is Ctrl-U.

25. The keyboard shortcut for Cut is Ctrl-X.

26. The keyboard shortcut for Paste is Ctrl-P.

27. Many Internet Service Providers will disconnect you when they do not see you actively sending or receiving information while connected on the Internet.

28. If you do not have an unlimited Internet plan, you can save connect time by writing your e-mails before you go online.

29. If you do not understand an option in a Windows dialog box, right-click the option, and in most cases you will see a "What's This?" button. Click on it to get help.

30. If you are viewing the contents of a floppy disk, and then insert a new disk into the floppy drive, you can view its contents by hitting the F5 button. This will refresh the contents of the open floppy disk window. The contents of the old disk will disappear from the window, replaced by the new one.

31. To copy a floppy disk, double-click on the My Computer icon. Right-click on the floppy disk icon. Choose Copy Disk from the pop-up screen.

32. When you see a letter underlined in a menu choice, it means that there is a keyboard shortcut for the item. Holding down the key marked "Alt" and pressing the underlined letter at the same time will produce the same results as clicking the mouse on the word.

33. A hotkey is a key or combination of keys such as Ctrl and an alphanumeric character that activate a pop-up program or cause some other predetermined action to occur.

34. If you pay online by credit card, your transactions will be protected by the Fair Credit Billing Act. Consumers have the right to dispute certain charges and temporarily withhold payment while the creditor investigates them.

35. Keep good records while shopping on the Internet. Print a copy of all purchase orders and confirmation numbers for your records. Read and print all e-mail messages a merchant sends you regarding your transaction.

36. When you enter a chat room, watch quietly in the background until you understand the nature of the conversation. Never give your full name, address, phone number or other personal information to anyone you meet in a chat room. Never reveal your social security number or credit card number to anyone in a chat room.

37. Make it a priority to download new versions of your browser when they are released.

38. When using a search function, a keyword is the word the user wants to find in a document.

39. To run a program effectively, it is best to have the recommended requirements instead of just the minimum requirements. Read carefully the requirements on the outside of the software package.

40. There is an additional piece of hardware for portable computers that allows you to use a laptop as both a portable and a desktop computer. It is called a docking station or port replicator. You slip the laptop into the docking station and it allows you to connect to accessories such as a keyboard and monitor.

41. Whenever you see "Press Any Key", remember that you can press any key you choose: x, y or z, the Spacebar, whatever you like. There is not an "any" key.

42. Do not print from a floppy. It usually takes a long time. It is better to copy the file to your hard drive and print from there.

43. Do not use magnets on or near your computer or floppies. If a magnet gets too close to a floppy or hard disk it will erase it.

44. Surge protectors cannot protect from lightning. In severe weather, unplug the entire computer system from the power and telephone lines to avoid damage to your PC.

45. You can find freeware and shareware at many Internet sites. Freeware programs are free to you. Shareware programs are provided for you to try without a cost. If you like the program, you can pay a small fee to register and continue using the program.

46. You can only cut, copy, and paste one text piece at a time. If you cut two segments in succession and then paste, you lose the first cut segment.

47. Keep your virus protection software up to date. Most virus protection updates are available through online services.

48. To view the date on your Desktop, move your mouse cursor over the time displayed in the far right corner of the Taskbar. The date will pop-up.

49. To install Accessibility options, click the Start button, then Control Panel. Double-click Add/Remove Programs, and then click the Windows Setup tab. Select the Accessibility Options check box, click OK, and then follow the instructions.

50. To pick a new color scheme for your Desktop, right-click the Desktop, choose Properties, then select the Appearance tab. Click the Scheme drop-down menu and choose a new color scheme.

51. To turn off your modem's speaker, go to the Control Panel and double-click the Modems icon. Click the General tab on the Modems property sheet. Select the appropriate modem. Click the Properties button. Click the General tab on this new property sheet, and move the slider control all the way to the left. Then click the OK button on each property sheet.

52. If you want to keep the Calculator handy, you can add it to the Windows Start Up group so it will run automatically at startup.

53. Right-click the shortcut properties for the Calculator to run it minimized on your Toolbar until you need it.

54. Look for a printer that has a lot of memory. More memory will allow it to print faster.

55. If you want to silence your PC, check the Mute All box under the first column in the Volume Control window.

56. You can adjust how quickly characters repeat as you hold down a key. Go to the Control Panel and double-click the Keyboard icon. Select the Speed tab and use the slider to adjust the cursor blink rate.

57. You can close an open window by pressing Alt-F4 instead of using your mouse.

58. Software piracy is the unauthorized copying of software.

59. A pixel is a cluster of colored dots that combine to form images on the computer screen.

60. A high-capacity drive is a floppy disk drive that can hold more information than the average floppy. They are slightly larger than regular floppy disks.

61. Cache is a small amount of computer memory that holds most recently used data.

62. Download only from trusted sources.

63. In a domain name, .com means a commercial (business) website. School sites have .edu and government sites have .gov endings.

64. Do not delete program files. If you want to get rid of a program, uninstall it through the Control Panel.

65. Keys with two characters on them give you the lower character. To get the upper character, press the Shift key.

66. Do not use the lower case L for the number one, or a capital O for zero. The computer is literal and treats them very differently.

67. To scroll continuously, hold the mouse button down instead of just clicking.

68. If you are buying a DVD (digital versatile disc) drive so that you can watch DVD movies on your PC, you need to make sure you have a multimedia computer.

69. When you purchase floppy disks, make sure that they are formatted for a PC. The disk box says they are Windows, IBM, or PC formatted. Do not buy disks formatted for a Mac. They will not work in your machine.

70. Clicking with the left mouse button will select any item.

71. Clicking with the right mouse button will give you information about the item or things that you can do with that item.

72. You can send anything to the Recycle Bin by highlighting it and pressing the Delete key or by dragging it to the Recycle Bin.

73. You can delete a shortcut (icon with a small arrow on it) without in any way affecting the program or folder itself.

74. When you delete files or programs, they stay in the Recycle Bin until you empty it. Items in the Recycle Bin take up space on your hard drive.

75. You can highlight any text or graphic by clicking your mouse on it or clicking the mouse button and holding it down while dragging across your intended selection.

76. You can drag any icon, file, or document to your Desktop for quick retrieval. Get into the habit of using your right mouse button to drag items.

77. When dragging with your right mouse button you are always presented with a choice. The computer will ask if you want to copy, move, or create a shortcut to the item.

78. FAQ stands for Frequently Asked Questions. It is a list of questions and answers you can review to familiarize yourself with the content.

79. Right-clicking your mouse on any icon, file, or folder will give you a useful menu, which has information about the object. This menu allows you to rename or delete the object and also can show you the object's properties.

80. In Windows, you can often do the same thing in several different ways. For instance, to save a file in most programs, click on the Save icon, choose Save from the File menu at the top of the screen, or hold down the Ctrl key and the s key, at the same time.

81. If you make changes to a file and save it again (without giving it a new name), the old file will be overwritten and only the file with the changes will remain on the disk.

82. You can drag any icon onto the Start button and drop it there. It will be added to the top of the Start menu so you can access it with two clicks instead of three or four.

83. When you save a file, it is written to whatever disk you choose, i.e. hard disk, floppy disk, etc. In most programs, you choose File, then Save. When the Save dialog box appears, be sure to note where the file is being saved. Click on the down arrow next to the Save In box to choose exactly where you want to put the file.

84. To avoid repetitive stress injuries sometimes associated with computer use (typing), you can buy a special ergonomic keyboard.

85. Most mail programs allow you to store frequently used addresses in an address book. You then look up the addresses in the address book rather than type them in each time. Be sure to put your backup copies in a safe place away from your computer. In case of some type of catastrophe, you will want our backup copies in a secure location.

86. If a program has an auto-save feature, you should turn it on and have it save frequently.

87. To rename a shortcut icon, right-click the icon, select the Rename command, type a new name, and press Enter.

88. To stop the screen saver and return to your program, press any key or move the mouse.

89. You can minimize the CD Player window, and the CD will continue to play.

90. If you are having a hard time locating icons on the Desktop, alphabetize them. Right-click the Desktop, Arrange Icons, and choose By Name. You can also arrange the icons by type, size, or date.

91. Dust your computer case and monitor at least once a week. If dust gets into the computer case, you could have problems. Do not use furniture polish on your electronics.

92. A slanted keyboard is easier to type on than a flat one. Most keyboards have adjustable legs on the underside that can be pulled into place so the end of the keyboard is higher.

93. Press Esc to cancel a command. The Esc key, in the upper left corner of your keyboard, lets you cancel commands and stop tasks that are underway.

94. If you need to select an entire paragraph in a document, position your cursor in the middle of the paragraph and triple-click.

95. If you seem to be typing over text instead of inserting new test, you may have depressed the Insert key. To deactivate Insert, simply press it again.

96. If you point to an underlined item and it does not turn dark, click the Desktop blotter icon (third from the Start button) on the Taskbar.

97. If your PC starts to slow down, your hard disk may be too full. If you use more than 85% of your hard disk's space, you may need to get rid of unneeded files, or you may need to add an additional hard disk.

98. In printing, the direction of the paper is called orientation. Portrait means that the paper is taller than it is wide. Landscape means the paper is wider than it is tall.

99. A newsgroup is often called a forum. It is an online discussion group where people exchange ideas about a common interest.

100. Usenet is a worldwide bulletin board system that can be accessed through the Internet or through many online services. It contains thousands of newsgroups.

101. An external hard drive makes backing up easy.

PART 5

Windows Vista Operating System

Vista

Vista, your Microsoft Windows operating system, offers more tools, buzzers, bells and advantages than older versions of the Windows operating systems.

There are different versions of Vista for business and home use. Most home users do not need a full-fledged business version of Vista.

There are compatibility issues between Vista and older hardware and software (programs written for Windows XP). You may have to buy new peripherals and upgrade some of your software when you start using Vista.

If you're just starting out with a new computer with Vista installed on it, this won't be a problem for you as everything will be new, so you can ignore the next section.

Upgrading From Windows XP To Vista

With the advent of Windows 7, the latest and greatest operating program from Microsoft, you might not want to upgrade to Vista. We at The Senior's Guide feel that upgrading an older computer to Vista just does not make much sense as computer hardware is relatively inexpensive and it will come with Windows 7.

However, if you do want Vista on your old machine, here's how to do it. First, there are minimum requirements of your current computer. They are:

- 1 GHz 32-bit (x86) or 64-bit (x64) processor
- 1 GB of system memory
- 40 GB hard drive with at least 15 GB of available space
- Support for DirectX 9 graphics with:
  - WDDM Driver
  - 128 MB of graphics memory (minimum)
  - Pixel Shader 2.0 in hardware
  - 32 bits per pixel
- DVD-ROM Drive
- Audio Output
- Internet access

Upgrade Advisor

The Upgrade Advisor is a Microsoft downloadable program that will scan your computer and give you a report on compatibility issues for both the system and devices on your current computer. It will also recommend solutions to these conflicts and recommend which version of Vista you should choose.

To start this process:

- Go to www.microsoft.com/windowsvista.
- Click on Get Ready.
- Click Windows Vista Upgrade Adviser.
- Download the Installer Package.
- Install the package and then run the scan.

You will receive a report on which versions of Vista you can run on your machine. You can purchase the version of Vista you want from many different retail outlets, both online and in stores. When you are ready to upgrade your computer to Vista, plan to take a few hours to do the work. Follow the instructions that will be included with your software purchase.

Depending on your hardware, and which version of XP you are using, you may have a lot of steps to accomplish to upgrade to Vista, including backing up all of your files to a safe place outside of your computer. For the most part, except for backing up your files, it is a simple matter of inserting the installation disc into your CD or DVD drive and following the on screen instructions.

If you go to Microsoft's Vista Website, you will notice they are really hoping you will purchase Windows 7.

Upgrading From Windows Vista To Windows 7

Please see the Windows 7 section of this book for the steps to upgrade your Vista machine to Windows 7. However, if you upgraded a XP machine to Vista, and now want to upgrade again, we at The Senior's Guide feel you should not upgrade an older machine to Windows 7.

The Welcome screen will be displayed to request your user sign-on details. If there are multiple users of a computer, the first screen you will see is a "user" selection screen. Each person will have their own settings for appearance, themes, choices and passwords. Select your user icon and your settings will appear.

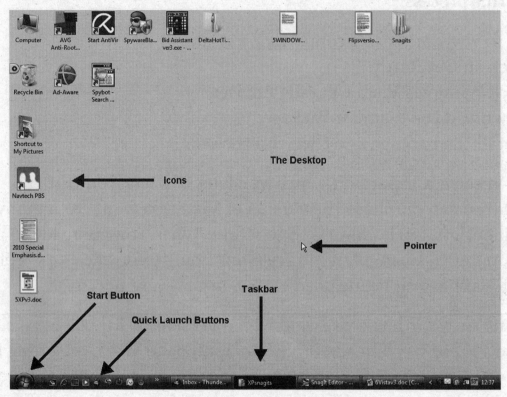

Figure 41: The Desktop

After the start-up, what you should see on the monitor is the Windows Desktop. It is your home base, like the physical desk where your computer sits. Several tools to get you started are placed on the background area. These include the Taskbar, sidebar, icons, and a Start button. If you have a fresh installation (not upgraded from a previous version) your Windows Vista Desktop should not have any icons except the Recycle Bin.

There will be variations from computer to computer on what the Desktop looks like. You will be able to customize the look of your Desktop to suit your artistic feelings.

Welcome Center

When you first start your computer, Microsoft has pre-programmed a Welcome Center to pop up as the first open window. The Vista Welcome Center is a great way to learn about your Vista computer and all you can do with it. There are tutorials that will teach you how to go onto the Internet, store photos, listen to music and much, much more.

It is also a great place to get help if you need any questions answered. Generally, every program has a help menu that you can do some research to solve any problems you are having.

When you no longer want to have the Welcome Center appear upon start-up, simply uncheck the box at the bottom of the screen that says not to show it at start up any more. You can always access the Welcome Center from the Start Menu.

Product Activation

When you first turn on your new computer, you will need to activate your Microsoft product. You will need to be able to go out onto the Internet to do this.

Product activation verifies that you have a valid copy of Vista and identifies you as the user. Once you are activated, you will have full use of Microsoft's Web sites to learn more about your computer and to keep it up to date with software improvements. This is important to keep your computer healthy and running trouble free.

Switching Users

If you have more than one user account defined on your computer, several accounts can be open at the same time. You don't have to close your programs and log off to be able to switch to another user. Switching between users is easy.

- Click the Start button.
- In the bottom right corner of the Start Menu, Click the Right Arrow.

- Now click Switch Users. A list of users will pop-up.
- Select your User Name.
- Insert your password.
- Either press Enter on the keyboard or click the arrow to the right of the password. Windows Vista will come up with all of your user settings and preferences.

Basic Controls And Mechanics

The Desktop

The Desktop is the working area (background) of the Windows display on your computer.

Look at your desk at home or work. It is the area where you do your paper-work. The Desktop of a computer is where you will pull out your electronic files, write electronic letters or work in your computer-based checkbook.

When you start your computer, you will see several screens go by before you arrive at the main Windows screen, which is the Desktop. The Desktop has three main parts: Taskbar, Start Menu, and icons.

Taskbar

Figure 42: The Entire Taskbar

The Taskbar is the horizontal bar along the bottom of the Desktop. It has the Start button on the left. Next to the Start button are the Quick Launch icons. Displayed in small rectangles near the middle of the Taskbar are the programs that are running. Near the right side, you will see the programs or tasks that start automatically when you start Windows. On the far right, you will see the time displayed.

Figure 43: Taskbar, Left Side

Figure 44: Taskbar, Middle

Figure 45: Taskbar, Right Side

The Taskbar allows you to start your navigation process through all of the computer files.

If you would like to move the Taskbar to another location, just move your cursor to the Taskbar, click and hold down the mouse button, and drag the Taskbar to another of the monitor's edges.

You can make a lot of changes to how the Taskbar works. Simply right-click on the Taskbar, select Properties from the dialog box and make all the adjustments you want to. In fact, for many facets of computing, a right-click will bring up dialog boxes that will have properties that you can adjust to enhance your computing experience.

Taskbar Buttons

The Taskbar Buttons launch programs in the same way as clicking on a Desktop icon.

The Start button is on the left side of the Taskbar. It has the Microsoft logo on it and if you place the pointer there, the word Start will appear.

Just to the right of the Start button are Quick Launch Buttons. These act like shortcuts to programs you use frequently.

For most buttons, if you hover your pointer over them, (that means put the pointer on the button, but don't press the mouse button) you'll get more information about what that button is.

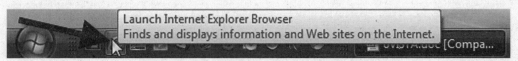

Figure 46: Hovering The Pointer

Task Manager

You can keep an eye on what is going on with your computer via the Task Manager. You can see what programs and processes are running, how much of your system resources are being used, monitor performance and close programs that are not responding. Here are two ways to get to the Task Manager:

1. Simultaneously press the Ctrl, Shift, Esc keys. The Task Manager will open up.

2. Simultaneously press the Ctrl, Alt, Delete keys. You will be taken to a screen that offers a number of choices. One is the Task Manager. Click that. This method is good to know if you want to log off your computer, change users or perform other tasks.

Taskbar Grouping

As you open programs and/or documents, the Taskbar can quickly become filled up with task buttons. To keep some semblance of order there, tasks that are using the same program will be grouped together with a number in the box to let you know how many are grouped there.

For example, if you run certain virus scanning software, three or four windows might be open at any one time. Meanwhile you might want to work on a document. As the Taskbar fills up with buttons, all of the virus software windows will be grouped under one name. The document and its program will be listed in another button. Open another document with the same program and it, too, will be grouped on the Taskbar.

You can see what is listed in each button by clicking on it. You can switch to any of those windows by clicking on the name of what you want.

Start Button And Start Menu

The Start button is the button that takes you almost everywhere in Windows. It is located on the Taskbar. Clicking on the Start button brings up a single menu from which many menus and programs can be accessed.

To display the Start Menu: Click the Start button. You will see the following window:

Figure 47: Start button Window

Start-Up Folder

The Start-Up folder will automatically start programs that you want running as soon as you turn on your computer. There are lots of programs that start when you turn on the computer, but this folder allows you to customize what you want.

For example, if you want the calculator turned on every time you start your computer, just follow these steps:

- Find the program you want, for our example, the calculator.
- Right-click on it and create a shortcut on the Desktop.
- Right-click the Start button.
- Select Explore.
- Select Start-Up.
- Drag the shortcut you created to the Start-Up folder.

Classic Start Menu

The Classic Start Menu looks like previous versions of Windows. Some folks feel more comfortable with what they are used to, so Microsoft includes that option in Vista.

The Classic Menu expands to the right as you click on choices in the Start Menu. The regular Vista Start Menu shows you the next level of choices in the Start Window itself.

To change from one to the other:

- Right-click the Start button.
- Select Properties.
- Check Classic if that is what you want.

Whether or not you are new to computers or upgrading from a previous version, we recommend using the new Vista version rather than the Classic version. There are more features for you with the new version that makes doing tasks easier.

Start Searches

Almost everything you might want to find through the Start Menu is available via the Start Search box. Simply start typing what you are looking for and a list will be displayed of all the possible choices based on what you have typed so far.

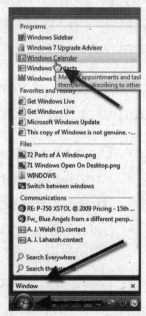

You can locate programs and data files just by typing in Start Search. When you find what you are looking for, click its name in the list. That program, or data file, will open.

The Classic Start View has no Start Search option. However, there is a simple way to find programs while in Classic mode:

Figure 48: Searching from the Start button

- Click on Start.
- Click on All Programs and a list of all the programs opens.

Pinning To The Start Menu

You will notice that on the Start Menu, on the left side, there is a top and bottom section. The top section is fixed. Those programs are *pinned* to the Start Menu and do not leave.

The bottom section is for recently used programs. These will change based on your usage.

However, if you would like to keep some of those programs in the upper "always there" section, you can pin them there.

To pin a program to the Start Menu:

- Right-click on the program.
- Select Pin To Start Menu. The program icon will shift to the upper section.

To unpin a selection:

- Right-click on a program in the pinned area.
- Select Unpin From Start Menu. The icon will leave the upper section.

Windows Sidebar And Gadgets

The Windows Sidebar is a vertical pane that holds small applications that you use frequently. These mini-apps are called Gadgets. There are hundreds of Gadgets available for your use from calculators to day/night clocks. Want your favorite news feed displayed? You can display that too.

To add a Gadget:

- Click the + sign at the top of the Sidebar or right-click anywhere in the Sidebar.
- Click Add Gadgets. A list will pop up of all of the available Gadgets.
- Select the ones that you want.

After you install a Gadget, you can customize each one to make them work better for you. You can move the Sidebar to a different location or even hide it when you do not want to see it. Right-click anywhere on the Sidebar for your choices.

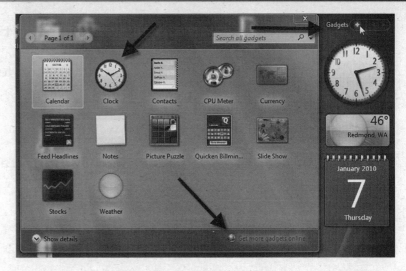

Figure 49: The Windows' Sidebar and Gadgets

Recent Items

Recent Items are files you have been working with lately. They might be individual letters, photos, documents, etc. Via the Start Menu, you can quickly see a list of those Recent Items and open them.

To see that list:

- Click on Start.
- From the list on the right side of the Start Menu, click Recent Items. A list of your recently looked at items will pop-up. Then click on the item you want and it will open.

Help And Support System

Not only can you get help from The Welcome Center, but Vista offers lots of help via the Help and Support Menu.

- Click on Start.
- Click Help and Support.

You will be taken to an area where you can find out information about how to use your computer, or solve a problem. Some of the help features require you to be able to go out onto the Internet. Make sure you are connected to the Internet before you try to find support out there.

Search Help

Search Help is a tool to quickly find the information you need to solve a problem.

- After you click Help and Support, a window appears and at the top is a rectangular typing box with "Search Help" in it.
- Place your curser there and type a topic you want to get help with.
- Press Enter on your keyboard.
- A list of possible solutions/answers to your question will appear in a new window. Click on one of the topics and you will be able to read about that topic.

Keep in mind that the computer help function cannot read minds. You may have to modify your request a bit until you get the information you are looking for.

Guided Help

Once you ask for help, you may get more than just information. You may get the steps to solve your issue. Simply click on the links as they come up (words highlighted in blue) and follow the instructions.

Sometimes, you are offered an automatic solution to your problem. The computer will fix the issue for you. For the most part, these automatic fixes work great. During this process, you may be asked questions pertaining to your issue. Once again, the computer is not a mind reader. It is just looking for information from you so it can apply the best solution.

Shutting Down

There are two ways to shut down your computer. You can put it to sleep, or you can completely power it down. To put your computer to sleep:

- Click the Start button.
- Click the Start Menu power button. (That's the split-circle image on the brown button to the right of the Search Box). Your work is saved, the display turns off and the computer goes into sleep mode. This allows you to quickly resume work when you get back to your computer.

To completely shut down your computer with a complete power-off:

- Select Start.
- Press the little arrow that is to the right of the brown sleep button.
- From the pop-up menu, select Shut Down. Notice you have other options from this menu including Sleep and Restart.

Frozen Computer

Every once in a while your PC may experience a puzzling failure. It may just freeze up for no reason at all. **DO NOT WORRY. YOU DID NOT DO IT!** It is just the nature of computers to get confused on occasion. When this happens, your mouse will stop responding, the keyboard is not functional and the computer just sits and stares at you. That pesky machine just won't respond to your inputs. You will need to restart the computer.

First, try to shutdown the frozen program:

- Click the Close [X] button in the right-hand corner of the window.
- If that does not work, press these three keys at the same time: Ctrl, Alt and Del.
- Find the frozen program in the list, select it and click End Program. The notation may say "Program Not Responding".
- If that did not work, click the Start button.
- Click the lower right arrow, then Restart.
- If that did not work, an alternate method is to press and hold the Ctrl and Alt keys, then press the Del key three times.
- If that did not work, here's the last ditch method. Turn off the power button on the computer. Let it rest for a minute or so and then turn it back on. On a number of computers, you must hold in the power button until the computer shuts down.

Another reason you might need to restart a computer is if you have loaded a new program. Sometimes Windows requires a restart for all the new settings to take effect. In this case, just use the Start Menu Restart procedure. Sometimes, the new program will offer to restart the computer for you.

Moving A Window

You may want to rearrange where a window is located on your Desktop. Follow these steps to move a window:

- Place the pointer on the window's title bar.
- Drag the title bar to the location you want and release the mouse button.

This will not work if your window is in full screen mode. Full screen means this one window takes up all the space on your monitor. You have to reduce the size of the window in order to be able to move it around.

In many Microsoft programs, rather than File being displayed in the upper left toolbar, a Microsoft logo is displayed. Many functions that we used to find under File will be found there.

Figure 50: Microsoft Logo "File" Button

Switching Between Windows

To look at a window that is not on top of the stack:

- Click on the window you want.
- Click on its Taskbar button or click on the Aero Quick Launch button. (A new feature of Vista is the Aero Button just to the right of the Start button. Clicking

Figure 51: Windows Aero Button

the Aero button allows you to easily switch between open windows on your Desktop, and then select the one you want to work with. It's a pretty cool shortcut to help you keep organized while you are working. Not all versions of Vista have the Aero button.)
- Select the window you want.
- When you select the window by any of these methods, the window will jump to the top of the stack.

Too Many Open Windows?

There are some commands you can use to "clean-up" the window clutter on your Desktop. If you have too many open windows:

- Right-click the mouse anywhere on the Taskbar and a menu appears.
- Select Cascade Windows. The Cascade command displays the windows so that the title bars of each window appear.
- Click on any title bar to bring its window to the front of each stack.
- Show Windows Stacked displays each window in horizontal panes and the Show Windows Side by Side displays each window in vertical panes.
- Click the Aero Quick Launch button to stack the windows for easy viewing.

You should always close a window once you are finished working with it. This will really help tame Desktop clutter.

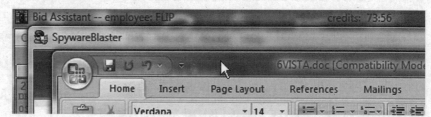

Figure 52: Cascading Windows

Using Menus And Sub-Menus

It is as simple as this:

- On the menu bar, choose the category of the command that you want. The menu opens.
- Click on the command you want.

If a sub-menu opens, it is just giving you more options of how to accomplish your task at hand. Find what you want and once again click on it.

Shortcut Menus

A shortcut menu or alternate menu is a hidden menu that can be shown with a right-click of the mouse. Almost every object on your computer has one. These are frequently used commands that are made easy to get to with one right-click.

The commands vary from program to program so you should right-click in every program you use to get an idea of what commands are at "your fingertips".

Vista Tasks

Finding Files And Folders

When you are looking for a particular folder or file, and you are not sure where it is located on your computer, you can use the Search command instead of opening numerous folders. The Search command lets you quickly search a specific drive or your entire computer.

To find a file or folder:

- Click the Start button, click on Start Search. The Search dialog box appears.
- In the Search box on the right, type the file or folder name you want to find.

You can narrow down the search by using the Show Only search bar.

- Click that category if you want to only show those results.
- Press Enter. The results of the search will appear. You can use Advanced Search if you want to tailor your search results.

A word to the wise: start filing your information in an orderly manner at the beginning of your computer experience. It will make life easier!

Opening A File Or Folder

After you have located the file you want, either through a search or by going straight to it in a directory, you can double-click on it to open it.

To find and open a file or folder without using Search:

- On the Desktop, double-click Computer.
- Double-click the drive that contains the file or folder you want to open.
- Double-click the file or folder.

If you have recently opened a file that you want to look at again, check Documents or Recent. You can also open files and folders from the File Open command in the application itself. For example, if you are working in Microsoft Word, you can find other Word created documents by using the File Open method. A list of your Word documents will show up.

Creating A File Or Folder

To create a folder:

- On the Desktop, double-click Computer.
- Double-click the disk drive or folder in which you want to create a folder. The drive or folder opens.
- On the Organize menu, click Create New Folder.

An alternate way is to:

Right-click a blank area on the Desktop.

- Click New.
- Click Folder and it will appear.
- While the "New Folder" title is highlighted, type a folder name of your choice and then press Enter.
- If you do not want the new folder to reside on the Desktop, drag it to the location you want it to move to.

Naming A File Or Folder

If you're saving something for the first time, Vista asks you to name the file or document. Type something descriptive. Use only letters, numbers, and spaces between the words. You can't use any of the following characters: : / \ * | < > ? "

The last three or four letters (suffix) of a file name designate an extension. An extension identifies the format of the file. It is preceded by a period.

Every file is in a specific format. There are many different formats. By naming a file with an extension, you tell the computer which format the file is in. That way the computer knows what format to use each time you want to work with that file.

Most programs automatically add the extension suffix when you save your work. For example, Microsoft Word documents end with the file extension .doc while Microsoft Excel spreadsheets end with the extension .xls. Newer versions of Microsoft Word save files as .docx. If you need to have your document read on an older machine, make sure you save it as a .doc, not a .docx. You can choose this when you save your work.

File Properties

File properties are the attributes of a particular file. This includes location, size, date created and much, much more.

To access any file's Properties box:

- Right-click on the file's icon, or if the file is open, click on the File menu.
- Click Properties. After Clicking Properties, the File Properties Box Opens.

Renaming A File Or Folder

It is simple to rename a file or folder. To rename:

- In a window, select the file or folder you want to rename. On the Organize menu, click Rename.
- Type a name and press Enter.

Or

- Select the file or folder you want to rename.
- Right-click on it and select Rename from the shortcut menu.
- Type a name and press Enter.

Be careful about renaming your files without thinking about it first. Shortcuts that use an old file name will no longer work. If you have linked a file to a program with an old name, the link will no longer work.

File conflicts exist when you try to name two different files with the same name. If you are creating the second file, Vista will warn you when you try to save a file name that already exists. Vista will offer three possible solutions:

- Copy and Replace.
- Don't Copy.
- Copy But Keep Both Files. Make sure you read the selections and pick the one that is most appropriate for what you want.

You should normally name each file with separate, specific names. For example, a lettertoson.doc should not be used for every letter to your son. The next letter could be lettertoson2.doc, lettertoson3.doc etc. If you make a copy of the file named lettertoson.doc, the copy will be titled lettertoson.doc (copy1). That way you can have this one letter appear as different files.

Copying Or Moving A File Or Folder

There are two simple ways to copy or move files and folders. To copy a file or folder:

- Right-click on a file or folder.
- Select Copy.
- Go to where you want the copy to appear and right-click.
- Select Paste. A copy of the original folder will appear.

To move a file or folder:

- Right-click the file or folder.
- Click Send To.
- Select from the list of likely locations.

You can also move a file by dragging its icon from one location to another:

- Open the folder that holds your file or folder that you want to move.
- Also open the destination folder.
- Re-size both windows so they both appear on your Desktop.
- Click on the target file or folder, hold down the mouse button and drag it to the destination folder. The icon will disappear from the original folder and appear in the new folder.

Folder Options

You can change how you see your folders just as you can modify your Desktop. You get choices everywhere with Windows Vista!

- Open a folder.
- Click on Organize. A Folder Options dialog box opens. From here you can make adjustments to how your folders look and act.

For both sorting and folder options, you will need to play around a bit. One recommendation is to click on Show Hidden Files and Folders. You never know when you are going to need to find something that is normally hidden. It's a good idea to be set up for it now.

Viewing Folders

There are a number of ways to look at each and every document, file or folder. You control this with the View Menu. For example, you might want your photos in a large icon format. This will give you a preview of each of your photos while still in the folder view. For documents, you may want a title list instead. You can choose your views for each and every folder from the View menu.

To change how you view inside any folder:

- Click on the View Tab on the toolbar.
- Adjust the settings as necessary.

Customizing Folders

You can "dress up" your folders by adding a picture or icon to any folder.

- Simply find a folder you want to customize.
- Right-click on a blank spot of the folder.
- Click Customize. A dialog box will appear so you can browse your computer and place a picture on the folder cover.

Once again, you'll need to play around a bit to get used to "massaging" your computer to the way you want it.

Compressed Folders

Compressed folders hold files that have been reduced in size so they take up less room on your disks. They are known as "zipped" folders and have a little zipper on the icon. These folders have not lost any important information from your files, but through some "propeller head" technology, they've squeezed the files down in size as you would a sponge.

Most users do not need to compress files and folders. However, if you find you need to, read on.

To compress files:

- Create a new compressed folder by right-clicking on an empty area of the Desktop.
- Click New Compressed (zipped) Folder. A new folder will appear.
- Name this new folder.
- Drag your files that you want to compress to this new folder. Now they're compressed.

To get them back from being compressed, just drag them to a non-compressed folder and they will come back. However, a compressed copy will remain in the compressed folder.

If someone sends you a compressed file, simply drag it out of the compressed folder and it will "reconstitute" itself. Again, most folks will not need to compress files.

Sorting Folders

While working in Windows Vista, you can sort folders in a number of different ways. By looking at the header bar, you will see various criteria that Windows can sort by. Want to see the folder list of when you last worked in the folders?

- Click Sort via the Date Modified header.

Want a reverse alphabetical listing?

- Click the Name header.
- Click the arrow to change from ascending to descending (or back).

Deleting A File Or Folder

To delete a file or folder:

- Right-click on the icon.
- Select Delete. This will send the file or folder to the Recycle Bin. Alternately, you can click on the icon and drag it to the Recycle Bin.

Customizing The Desktop

You can change the appearance to suit your desires. You can move icons around, remove icons, add icons, change the colors and so much more.

If you don't like the standard color scheme on your Desktop, you can change it. You can use pre-defined color schemes or make up your own. If your color selections are too wild they may cause eye strain!

- Right-click on an empty portion of the Desktop.
- A pop-up menu appears. Click on Personalize and you will be given a number of tabs to make changes.

Some folks worry that they'll make a change that "ruins" their computer. Don't worry. Play around a bit. You can always put things back the way they were.

Arranging Icons

You can arrange your icons any way you want.

- Put your pointer on each icon you want to move.
- Click and hold down the left mouse button and drag the icons where you want them. Then release the button.
- On a blank spot on the Desktop, right-click the mouse.
- Select View and then un-check Auto Arrange and Align to Grid. Your icons should stay put.

- By clicking Auto Arrange, the computer will put them where it thinks they should go. With Align to Grid, they will be stacked neatly on the Desktop.

I like to put my anti-virus icons on the right side to remind me to run my scans. I keep the documents that I am working on in the middle of the Desktop. I keep the Computer, Recycle Bin and other frequently used icons on the left side.

Playing A CD

Playing music with the CD Player is very simple. A feature called auto-play detects when you insert a CD into the CD drive and automatically starts the music for you.

If auto-play does not work, here is how to do it manually:

- Click the Start button.
- Select All Programs.
- Select Windows Media Player.
- Select the CD title in the list on the left.
- Select the song title in the right pane.

You do not have to use Windows Media Player. If you have a different player on your computer, follow their instructions for their product. Other players include iTunes, Real Player and Adobe Media Player, just to name a few.

An alternative to the alternative is to double-click the Computer icon. Then double-click the drive you inserted the CD in. When you click a track, your default media player will play the music.

Playing Media Clips And Movies

Playing any media format is easy with Windows Media Player.

- Open the player as you did on the previous page by going to Start.
- Click All Programs.
- Click Windows Media Player (or click the Windows Media Player icon).
- On the File menu, click Open.

- Browse and locate the file you want to view or hear.
- Click on that and it should start playing.

If you receive a media file via e-mail, it probably played just fine when you clicked on it. However, if you try to find it while it is still in your e-mail inbox via a media player, you might not find it. If this happens: save the media file to a folder outside of your e-mail program.

Windows Media Center

This is a more advanced version of Windows Media Player, but is only offered with Vista Home Premium and Ultimate editions.

Not only can you play CDs and DVDs, but Windows Media Center will catalog all digital media content on your computer to give you a one-stop viewing location for videos, movies, photos and much more. In addition, with the correct hardware added, you can listen to FM radio broadcasts and even watch TV on your computer monitor. When you first start Windows Media Center, you will need to run a setup program. Express Setup works best for most users.

Screen Saver

A screen saver is a program that displays an image or animation on your screen when your PC is idle.

It was invented to ensure that all parts of the monitor screen received equal amounts of illumination so a ghost image would not be "burned" onto the screen. Today's monitors don't have burn-in problems and screen savers are not really necessary, but almost everyone uses them anyway.

Screen savers are fun and often entertaining. You can use any number of pre-installed screen savers or you can use screen savers downloaded from the Internet. You can even use any of your saved digital photos.

Vista comes with many screen savers as part of the package. There are many more screen savers available commercially.

To find the screen savers included with Vista:

- Right-click on a blank spot on the Desktop.
- Select Personalize to open the display properties dialog box.
- On the Screen Saver link, select an option from the drop-down list.
- Click OK to make this your screen saver.

To use images you have stored on your computer as your screen saver, simply pick Photos as your screen saver option.

Burn To Disc

To burn a disc simply means to make a copy. You could be copying music from your computer to a CD so you can play some tunes in your car. You could also be backing up your checkbook files. This is also known as burning. The term is used whether you are copying to a CD or DVD.

Vista makes it easy to burn files:

- First, make sure you have the correct discs for the type of drive you have. You cannot burn a DVD in a CD drive.
- Select the file you want to copy.
- Click on the Burn button on the toolbar. Follow the instructions.

Recycle Bin

The Recycle Bin is just another folder that holds the files and folders you want to permanently delete. However, just like the trash at home, you have to "take it out" to really get rid of them.

Figure 53: Recycle Bin

Until you empty the Recycle Bin, the files and folders can be moved back to wherever you want them. This way you do not have to worry about sending things to the recycle bin and then wondering if you should not have thrown them out.

When you delete files and folders from your hard disk drive they are moved to the Recycle Bin. However, files and folders that you delete from the Command Prompt don't go into the Recycle Bin. For example, if you start working on a document and don't save it, and then you close the window, your work will not be saved and it will not appear in the Recycle Bin, it is simply deleted.

To get something out of the Recycle Bin:

- Click on the Recycle Bin Icon.
- Either click on Restore All or right-click on an individual file or folder.
- Select Restore. The file or folder will be restored to your Desktop.

Program Buttons

Program Buttons appear on the middle of the Taskbar to identify any open applications or programs currently being used along with the documents you are working on. On the right side of the Taskbar you will see programs that start automatically when you start Windows. On the far right you will see the time displayed.

If a program is minimized (meaning it does not appear on the screen, but is still running), clicking on it from the Taskbar brings it back on-screen. You can easily switch to a different window by clicking its program button on the Taskbar.

Removing A Program

The best way to uninstall a program is by using the Programs and Features icon, located in the Control Panel.

It is not a good idea to simply delete the program folder from Computer Icon or Windows Explorer. The original program installation may have put files in other folders and changed some of the system settings.

To remove a program:

- Click the Start button.
- Select the Control Panel.
- Double-click the Programs and Features icon.
- Select the program you want to uninstall.
- Select Uninstall. There are two other options in this dialog box: Change or Repair. You will rarely use them.

Windows Explorer is a method of seeing everything on your computer. You look at the contents through a single window in a hierarchical structure.

Figure 54: Windows Explorer

The left side of the Windows Explorer window contains a list of your drives and folders, and the right side displays the contents of any folder you select from the left side list. You can use View in the upper tool bar to change how the icons on the right half of the window appear. To use Windows Explorer:

- Click the Start button.
- Select All Programs.
- Click Accessories.
- Click Windows Explorer.
- In the left pane, click the letter that represents your hard drive. The hard drive contents will appear in the right pane.

Looking At Folders Inside Windows Explorer

When you start working with Windows Explorer, you will be looking at folders. When you click on a folder, you will be looking at the folders inside that folder. You continue to look down into the filing structure until you find the file you want to work with. This might be a document, a photo or a music file. To the computer, they are all the same: just files.

Once you find the file you are looking for, you can easily see where it is located by looking at the Address Bar.

Address Bar

The Address Bar displays the location "trail" for your file. It shows the file's location in hierarchal format all the way back to the hard drive. But it also allows you to jump to any of the locations displayed in the address bar. In the following picture, if you clicked on Documents, you would be shown a list of files in the Documents Folder. Click on one of those, and you will go there.

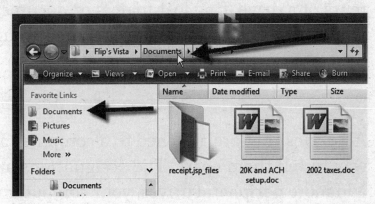

Figure 55: Using The Address Bar To Open Files

Computer Icon

The Computer Icon (labeled My Computer in earlier Windows versions) is another way to view the entire contents of your computer. It allows you to browse drives, directories (folders) and files.

Figure 56: Computer Icon

Unlike Windows Explorer which shows you the contents in a hierarchical structure, clicking on the Computer Icon shows you the contents of a single folder or drive.

For example, if you click on the Computer Icon either on the Desktop or in the Start Menu, you will see the next level of folders and files that are stored there. That level includes your hard drive, your removable drives and maybe a few folders. Obviously your computer holds more than that.

Click on the hard drive and now you see the contents of the hard drive. Keep working through your drive until you find the folder or file you want.

Exploring My Drives

It does not matter whether you look through your drives via Windows Explorer or the Computer icon. You will get the same results. However, you will gravitate to the method you like best.

The reason you may want to look through the drives is to see the entire contents of a drive, find lost folders or documents, or move files around. There is a lot you can accomplish by looking through the filing architecture of your computer.

Differences Between Drives

All drives that are attached to a computer are assigned a letter. It's a simple way to tell them apart. The designations are A:, B:, C:, D:, E:, F: etc. As you add more peripheral drives, your computer will automatically assign them a letter.

In the past, the A: drive was for the floppy drive. The B: drive was for a second floppy. The C: drive was the computer's main hard drive. Even though your computer may not have any floppies, by convention, most computers' hard drives are the C: drive. If your com-

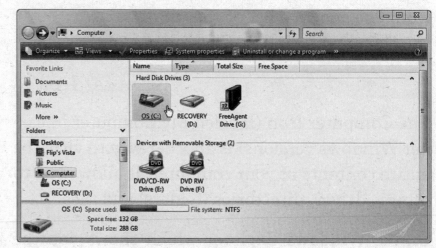

Figure 57: Drive Lettering

puter came with a second installed hard drive, or partitioned your only hard drive into two parts, the second hard drive or part will be the D: drive.

You can see all the drives connected to your computer by clicking on the Computer icon.

Windows Update Feature

Windows Update is a service provided by Microsoft to keep your computer in tip top condition, software wise. It will install updates to Windows and other Microsoft programs, patches for problems that arise in Microsoft programs and help keep your computer secure and performing well.

You can elect to let Microsoft update your computer automatically, or just inform you that updates are available. At The Senior's Guide, we recommend that you use the automatic feature. This means once again you should leave your computer on when you schedule Windows to update.

To set up Windows Update:

- Click the Start button.
- Type Update in the Search Box.
- Click on Windows Update in the Start Menu. The main window tells you the status of Windows Update. If this is your first time going to Windows Update, you should update your computer right away.

System Properties

Want to find out more about your computer details? You can check your system properties at any time.

- Right-click the Computer Icon on your Desktop.
- Click Properties. You will get a box chock full of information about your computer.

There are other ways of finding this same information. You can go to the Control Panel and click on System and Maintenance. In the Welcome Center, simply click View Computer Details. You might need to find this page if you are working with tech support people to solve a problem.

PC Performance Information

Microsoft gives you tools to see how well your computer is performing against the 'benchmark' Windows system. To see how well your computer is performing:

- Open the System Properties box as described above.
- Click Performance in the lower left corner of the box.

A new screen will open showing you various scores for system components. This is a relative scoring system and you do not need to pay much attention to it unless you are unhappy with your computer's overall performance.

From this page, you can find out information on how to improve performance in various areas. Sometimes it just requires a little housekeeping. Other solutions require spending money. Unless you absolutely have to, don't spend extra money for computer improvements that may not give you much more performance.

Disk Clean Up

Disk Clean Up is a utility function that removes unnecessary files from your computer. This should be considered a good housekeeping tool and should be done frequently. This will help keep your performance high.

To run Disk Clean Up:

- Go to the Performance section.
- Right-click on Computer.
- Click Properties, click Performance.
- In the left menu, click Open Disk Clean Up.
- Select the drive you want to clean and click on OK. (It may take a few minutes to discover all that can be deleted.)
- When shown the results, make sure all the boxes are checked.
- Click OK. All the files will be permanently deleted.

Defragging

Computers store information in clusters. However, the clusters of one file may not all be stored in the same area of the hard drive. This is normal and over time, the hard drive's ability to retrieve these clusters slows down as more and more clusters are farther and farther apart. When this happens, the disk is fragmented.

To improve performance, you can straighten up the disk and put the files back in order. This is known as defragging.

To defrag your disk:

- Click Start.
- Type in the search box Disk Defrag or just Defrag. The Disk Defragmenter dialog box will open up.

- To defrag right now, click the Defragment Now button.

You will notice an area of this box that allows you to schedule Defrags for the future. See the next topic for more information.

Scheduling Maintenance Tasks

While in the Defrag box, you can set up a schedule for future defrags. Choose a time when no one is using the computer and the computer will be on. I usually use one or two o'clock in the morning. Yes, that means I leave my computer on overnight.

To set up future defrags:

- Click the Modify Schedule button in the Disk Defragmenter box. Adjust the time and dates.
- Click OK.

To schedule other tasks, including maintenance tasks:

- Click Start.
- Type in the Search Box "Task Scheduler".
- Click Task Schedule in the Start list. Follow the instructions within the boxes.

There are many things you can schedule with Task Scheduler. You can even remind yourself to take your daily vitamins!

Backing Up

The best back-up method is the one that you do! I'm not trying to be flippant; backing up is important. If you back up irregularly, you are at risk of losing the information stored on your computer. If the information is not important to you, or is easily replaced from paper files, then you do not have to worry about backing up. However, most of us need the information on our computers. Daily!

I like backing up to an external hard drive. However, not everyone has one. Backing up your files to disk is fairly easy.

- Click on Start.
- Type in the Search Box "Backup".
- Click Backup And Restore Center from the top of the list.
- Click Backup files.

If you are using CD or DVD discs, make sure you have the appropriate kind for your drive, and plenty of them. Follow the on-screen directions pertaining to drive selection and start times.

Windows Security System

The Windows Security System in Vista is a comprehensive safety tool to keep your computer free from viruses, malicious software, intentional intrusions and all the bad stuff out on the Internet. It's not foolproof, but it is the first line of defense in your computer.

To go to the Security Center:

- Click on Start.
- Click on Control Panel.
- Click on Security Center. You can also type Security Center in the Start Search Box.

Items marked in green are deemed okay. In red, yellow or orange, some attention is needed. The areas addressed here are Windows Firewall, Windows Defender, Windows Update and Internet Options. Windows Defender is the heart of the security system. Make sure you use Windows Defender all the time.

Windows Firewall

A firewall keeps intruders out of your computer. You should always have one turned on. Vista has its own firewall and you should use it if you do not have another one. If you have another firewall that you want to use, great! Install it and turn it on. However, you should turn the Vista firewall off. Two firewalls running at the same time will not work well together.

From the Windows Security Center:

- Click Windows Firewall to change settings.
- Turn it on or off, or to allow exceptions to get through the firewall. The exceptions tab is rarely used for most home users so you should not have to deal with this.

Malware Protection

Malware harms your computer. Malware is defined as malicious software. It is software that you do not want on your computer. It generally comes via e-mail that you download onto your computer.

Malware is further delineated as spyware, adware, viruses, Trojans and any number of other nomenclature designations that will be created in the future.

Windows Defender is Vista's weapon against spyware and adware. It is automatically turned on when you turn on your computer. Windows Defender scans your computer for malware infections. By default, Windows Defender scans your computer at 2 AM. This is a good reason to keep your computer on overnight. However, from the Tools menu in Windows Defender, you can adjust the scan time to suit your schedule.

In the left hand section of the window are some links. Change Settings is where you can customize how Windows Update works. You can elect not to update (NOT RECOMMENDED!), inform you of updates and allow you to select the ones you want, or update automatically and at what time, and how often.

1. You can save your progress in most of the games included with Windows Vista.

2. You can create XML documents, which are more secure than regular text files or even word processor docs. Just create a document in a word processor, print it via the options menu, and select the XPS printer.

3. File names and folder names can be very long, but they can't contain the following characters: \ / : * ? " < > |.

4. Files and folders on floppy drives, key drives, and network drives are really deleted when you delete them. The Recycle Bin doesn't work on floppies, key drives, or drives attached to other computers on your network.

5. Shadow copies are also called previous versions or back-up copies of your data files, which Vista keeps for you automatically. However, if you have Vista home or Vista Home Premium, you don't get shadow copies protection.

6. If you choose a CD or DVD drive for automatic back-ups, you need to remember to put a blank CD or DVD in the drive before the backup runs.

7. Windows Vista games deposit their saves into a special directory, called Saved Games, in your personal folder. In theory, that will make upgrading to a new system much easier for gamers, who like to migrate their game saves.

8. When using the Help system, it's usually advantageous to include Microsoft's online database in your search. The online/offline status of your search is located on the bottom right of the Help window.

9. The Games folder is a powerful repository of all things gaming. From within, you launch games, update games with the latest patches, enable parental controls to protect younger users from harmful content, and more. Invoke it by clicking Start/Games.

10. Do you use the icon in the upper left corner of system and application windows? A quick double-click closes the window (instead of a single click on the X at the upper right). Though Microsoft left the icon out in Vista, the function remains.

11. In Microsoft Windows Explorer, you can use column headers (Name, Size, and so on) to sort files. Savvy users may right-click on a column head to remove items or add some — say, Dimensions for images. There are around 45 such columns available in Windows XP. Windows Vista has well over 250, covering a multitude of metadata.

12. The new Program Menu shows you only recently used applications and requires extra clicks to navigate to submenus. This can be very frustrating but, thankfully, the Search box Microsoft has added to the Start Menu is a great replacement. As quickly as you can type, it returns intelligent results in apps, files, even e-mail messages.

13. Unlike previous versions of Windows, Vista's Task Scheduler wakes up a PC that's suspended or hibernating, runs the scheduled task, and then puts the PC back to sleep.

14. Previous versions of Windows provided Outlook Express to support the e-mail functions. In Windows Vista, this is replaced by Windows Mail.

15. For e-mail, click the box to ask Windows Mail to remember the password, so you don't have to enter it each time you send or receive mail.

16. The windows Contacts folder replaces the Windows Address Book found in previous versions of Windows.

17. Marking a message as not junk will move that message to your Inbox, but future messages from that sender might still end up in the junk e-mail folder.

18. The Windows Security Center has an irritating habit of not properly identifying installed software.

19. You can remove an icon from the Windows Desktop by right-clicking it and choosing Delete, or by clicking it once and pressing Delete.

20. Task Manager: Press Ctrl+Shift+Esc.

21. Tasks Screen: Press Ctrl+Alt+Del.

22. To launch the shortcuts on the Quick Launch toolbar: Press Windows logo key + 1-0.

23. To cycle through programs on Taskbar: Press Windows logo key + T.

24. To bring all gadgets to the front and select windows Sidebar: Press Windows logo key + Spacebar.

25. To cycle through Sidebar gadgets: Press Windows logo key + G.

26. To open Windows Mobility Center: Press Windows logo key + X.

27. To open a folder, press and release Alt to show the Menu Bar (also works in Internet Explorer).

28. You can speed up your PC on the fly by simply plugging in a USB drive (or iPod or Compact Flash card or any external drive) with some spare megabytes.

29. You can find the Command bar just below the Address bar and here you can start different activities, depending on the files that are contained in the folder you are currently in. Therefore, if you access a folder with images, you have the option to open the pictures with Windows Photo Gallery, send them through e-mail or Burn a pictures CD.

30. Navigation Pane: this pane contains two sections: Favorite links — that provides access to some of your favorite links like Documents and Pictures — and Folders, which displays the location you are currently browsing.

31. Details Pane: detailed information (Date Modified, Authis, Size) about a certain file or folder is displayed in the Details Pane. You can also add you own tags and your own categories, which can help you when searching for that specific file/folder.

32. Preview Pane is located on the right hand side and it allows you to view the content of a file without opening it.

33. Command Bar gives you the option to Organize your files and folders, change the View and even Print or Burn a file/folder on a CD/DVD. Address Bar displays the location you are currently in and you can also type a URL and have the Explorer display a Web page.

34. Search Box allows you to search files and folders on your computer.

35. Every anti-spyware application (free or paid) MUST have the following features: 1. Effective real time protection against all spyware-related threats that may attack your computer. 2. The backup and restore functions are vital necessities. 3. Automatic updates are a must, also. 4. Detailed scanning results and descriptions of encountered problems. 5. The ability to completely remove all files, directories and registry entries associated with a certain spyware threat. 6. Easy to install and use for every average computer user. 7. Scheduled scanning is another feature worth its weight in gold. 8. The ability to set scanning options manually, and also have access to quick and full scan modes.

36. Pressing F1 opens Help information in most programs.

37. To avoid problems, close all open programs before starting any program installation.

38. A zip drive is a type of disk with a higher density than a floppy disk. You can store more information on it than a floppy disk.

39. To rename a shortcut icon, simply right-click the icon, select Rename, and type in a new name. Press enter.

40. If you subscribe to an online mailing list, be sure you know how to unsubscribe.

41. When describing a CD or DVD, the term "disc" is used instead of "disk." They are pronounced the same.

42. Changing the magnification on your screen only changes the way text appears. Zooming in (and out) doesn't physically alter the text itself.

43. Undo command: Ctrl + Z.

44. Redo command: Ctrl + Y.

45. Cut: Ctrl + X, Copy: Ctrl + C, Paste: Ctrl + V.

46. Save a file: Ctrl + S.

47. Check your spelling: F7.

48. If you don't want any home page — allowing your browser to appear on the screen faster — click the down arrow next to the Home icon, choose Remove, and click the home page.

49. As you hover over a drive or folder in the Folders list, it expands to reveal the subfolders.

50. The Cut command removes the selection. It turns gray until you Paste it. If you change your mind, put the cursor back and select Paste.

51. Files and folders that you delete from the Command Prompt, don't go into the Recycle Bin. Also, there's no recycle bin for drives with removable media.

52. Right-click the Recycle Bin icon and select Empty Recycle Bin, to remove all of the files and folders without it being open.

53. Compressed folders are distinguished from other folders by a zipper on the folder icon.

54. To create a compressed folder and copy a file into it at the same time: right-click a file, select Send To, Compressed (zipped) Folder. The new compressed folder has the same file name, but a file extension of .zip.

55. When you install new programs, their entries automatically appear under All Programs, positioned alphabetically, or in a new folder within All Programs.

56. Not all the Start Menu features and functions apply when you use the Classic Start Menu.

57. Press Alt + Enter to make the Command Prompt window full screen if it's windowed, or vice versa.

58. Mistyping a URL can display sites that take advantage of common typing errors to parody genuine Web sites, so be very careful.

59. You don't have to type the http:// prefix, since Internet Explorer will assume this and provide it automatically.

60. You can right-click any link in a Web page or in search results, and select Add to Favorites.

61. Web mail stores and retains your e-mail on a mail server. The main Web mail services are particularly subject to spam messages, although the service provider will usually detect and transfer such messages into a separate folder.

62. If you click and drag a file into the Photo Gallery window, the file gets copied to your Pictures folder — even if it isn't a picture file.

63. If you delete a photo from the Photo Gallery, Vista deletes the file — so the picture not only disappears from the Gallery, but it also disappears period. You can get it out of the Recycle Bin if it wasn't on a network drive.

64. Tags that you assign to a picture travel with the picture.

65. Make it a priority to download new versions of your browser when they are released.

66. When using a search function, a keyword is the word the user wants to find in a document.

67. Software piracy is the unauthorized copying of software.

68. Pixels are clusters of colored dots that combine to form images on the computer screen.

69. Cache is a small amount of computer memory that holds most recently used data.

70. Do not delete program files. If you want to get rid of a program, uninstall it.

71. Do not use the lower case L for the number one, or a capital O for zero. The computer is literal and treats them very differently.

72. To scroll continuously, hold the mouse button down instead of just clicking.

73. If you seem to be typing over text instead of inserting new text, you may have depressed the Insert key. To deactivate Insert, simply press it again.

74. In printing, the direction of the paper is called orientation. Portrait means that the paper is taller than it is wide. Landscape means the paper is wider than it is tall.

75. A newsgroup is often called a forum. It is an online discussion group where people exchange ideas about a common interest.

76. Malware (malicious software) is designed to deliberately harm your computer. To protect your system, you need up-to-date antivirus and anti-spyware software. Only the latter is provided as part of Windows, so you'll need a separate antivirus program.

77. Firewall is on by default in Windows Vista, but you can turn it off if you have another Firewall installed and active.

78. System Restore is not intended for personal data files.

79. The ability to set up automatic backups is not included in Windows Vista Starter and Windows Vista Home Basic editions.

80. To play DVDs you must have a DVD drive and a compatible DVD decoder, such as provided on systems that include Windows Media Center.

81. Some windows are fixed and cannot be resized. These include dialog boxes and applications, such as Windows Calculator.

82. Unless you specifically tell Windows Mail that you want it to download and show you pictures inside e-mail messages, it won't.

83. To cancel a document from printing, select that document. In the print queue window, choose Document, Cancel. Or, right-click the document in the print queue window and choose Cancel.

84. Copying from a CD is also known as ripping.

85. To add gadgets to the sidebar: Click the + at the top of the side bar. Drag the icon of the gadget you want to your side bar and the gadget will appear.

86. Ever wanted to talk to your computer? Click the Start Orb. Click Control Panel. Click Speech Recognition. Click Start Speech Recognition.

87. Leave your computer on for as long as you can. I leave my computer on for months on end. Every time I restart my computer, the cache to certain folders, files, etc. is deleted.

88. The Windows Firewall now has the option to configure incoming and outgoing traffic, which I think is great. It comes in very handy when you need it most.

89. Keep files organized. I keep all my pictures, videos, documents... everything is organized. I truly think it is very helpful to know where all your files and folders are. This way, they are also not thrown all over the place so you forget what you're looking for.

90. Delete software that you do not need from "Remove Programs."

91. Running Programs. Always check what programs/ processes you have running on your computer through the task manager. It usually helps because some programs will stop responding in the background if you have one that is taking up a huge amount of resources. You might experience some lag.

92. Windows Vista's Basic and Classic versions will interface with most graphics hardware that supports Windows XP.

93. When you run the Upgrade Advisor it will automatically update itself so that you get the latest changes.

94. Print or save the full report before exiting the Upgrade Advisor.

95. You can set Windows to accept a single-click instead of the default double-click.

96. If there are too many tasks to fit on the Taskbar, Windows will group like items together.

97. If you click the Help button in any folder, it will open the Help and Support Center positioned at a relevant topic.

98. Windows Vista's default power-off state is Sleep mode, which records the contents of memory to the hard disk (just like Hibernate) but also maintains the memory for a period of time (as in XP's Standby mode).

99. When you perform a search with Vista's new, instant search feature, you can save the search in a special folder. This powerful feature allows you to create a virtual folder which, by default, is saved in your \\Searches\ folder. Every time you open such a folder, the search results are updated.

100. In Windows Vista, you can add additional clocks to the system tray. Click the clock, and then click Date and Time Settings. Click the Additional Clocks tab. You can add one or two additional clocks to the tray and select their time zones.

101. Visit www.theseniorsguide.com and our sister site: www.MeAndMyCaregivers.com.

PART 6

Windows 7 Operating System

Windows 7 Operating System

Microsoft Windows (Windows, for short) is the name of the operating system that lets you give orders to your computer.

Windows 7 offers more tools, buzzers, bells and advantages than older versions of the Windows operating systems. It's main goal of fixing problems with Vista, and adding features equal to or better than Apple Mac's Snow Leopard, has been achieved.

There are different versions of Windows 7 for business and home use. Most home users do not need a full-fledged business version of Windows 7. You can save a few dollars by only buying the version you really need. The most often purchased versions of Windows 7 are: Windows 7 Home Premium, Windows 7 Professional and Windows 7 Ultimate. If you find you need to upgrade to Windows 7 Ultimate from either of the other two, it is a simple matter of paying for an unlock code through the Windows Anytime Upgrade program.

There are some compatibility issues between Windows 7 and older hardware and software (programs written for Windows XP). You may have to buy new peripherals and upgrade some of your software when you start using Windows 7.

If you're just starting out with a new computer with Windows 7 installed on it, this won't be a problem for you as everything will be new, so you can ignore the next section.

Upgrading Your Current Computer To Windows 7

Your first step will be to visit the Microsoft website and get the Upgrade Advisor. The Upgrade Advisor is a Microsoft downloadable program that will scan your computer and give you a report on compatibility issues for both the system and devices on your current computer. It will also recommend solutions to these conflicts and recommend which version of Windows 7 you should choose.

To start this process:

- Go to www.microsoft.com/windowsWindows 7.
- Click on Get Windows Windows 7 in the toolbar.
- Click on See if your PC can run Windows Windows 7. The link is on the right side of the screen.
- Download the Installer Package.
- Install the package and click Start Check to run the scan.

You will receive a report on which versions of Windows 7 you can run on your machine. You can purchase the version of Windows 7 you want from many different retail outlets, both online and in stores. When you are ready to upgrade your computer to Windows 7, plan to take a few hours to do the work. Follow the instructions that will be included with your software purchase. For the most part, except for backing up your files, it is a simple matter of inserting the installation disc into your CD or DVD drive and following the on screen instructions.

Upgrading From Windows XP To Windows 7

With the advent of Windows 7, the latest and greatest operating program from Microsoft, you might want to upgrade your old XP machine to Windows 7. We at The Senior's Guide feel that upgrading an older computer to Windows 7 just does not make much sense as computer hardware is relatively inexpensive and it will come with Windows 7. There are extra steps involved with upgrading from an XP machine that you do not have to do when upgrading from a Vista machine. And no, we do not recommend upgrading to Vista in order to upgrade to Windows 7. It will be easier, and no more expensive, to just buy a new low cost computer with Windows 7 on it.

However, if you do want Windows 7 on your old XP machine, first check that your current computer has these minimum system requirements:

- 1 GHz 32-bit (x86) or 64-bit (x64) processor
- 1 GB of system memory
- 40 GB hard drive with at least 15 GB of available space

- Support for DirectX 9 graphics with:
  - WDDM Driver
  - 128 MB of graphics memory (minimum)
  - Pixel Shader 2.0 in hardware
  - 32 bits per pixel
- DVD-ROM Drive
- Audio Output
- Internet access

We highly recommend viewing the tutorial at Microsoft if you are seriously interested in upgrading your XP machine. You can find out exactly how to make a successful upgrade by going to http://windows.microsoft.com/en-US/windows7/help/upgrading-from-windows-xp-to-windows-7

Upgrading From Windows Vista To Windows 7

After you have run the Upgrade Advisor on your Vista Machine, you will need to purchase an upgrade software package. Once you have those discs in hand, it is a simple process to upgrade your computer to Windows 7. I upgraded the laptop we are using to write this book and although it took a few hours for the entire process, it was glitch free.

That being said, you should do a few things before you install the Windows 7 package. Go to your computer manufacturer's website and update your BIOS. BIOS, according to Answers.com, are "routines stored in read-only memory that enable a computer to start the operating system and to communicate with the various devices in the system, such as disk drives, keyboard, monitor, printer, and communications ports." If you have old BIOS, although your computer works just fine, Windows 7 will ask you to get the latest BIOS from your manufacturer. So you might as well do this first.

After you have updated your BIOS, update all of your anti-virus and malware programs and run scans on your computer to know you are free of all of the menaces running around out in cyberland.

Now that you have a clean machine, insert the correct upgrade disc into your drive slot. The upgrade package will come with 32 bit and 64 bit discs. Pick the correct disc for your computer. Unless you have a real reason to run a 64 bit system, you should stay with a 32 bit computer. If you are running older programs, running a 64 bit system will force you into upgrading all of those older programs. And some programs, such as Microsoft Office, only work in a 32 bit environment.

Click the Install Now option and let the process run. You should not have to watch the process, answer questions or make choices from a dialog box. Go watch TV and check periodically to see if it's done.

After the installation, you may be asked for your language preference, country or region, a user name, password and a name for this computer if you are using it on a network. You will be asked for the Product Key that comes on a card in the software package. It is very important to put in the correct product key and to activate your software online. The product key is a 25 character key that is comprised of 5 groups of 5 letter and number characters. It is in the format of:

ABC12-DEF34-GHI56-JKL78-MNO90.

Keep in mind that the letter I and the numeral 1 are not interchangeable in the computer world. Nor is the letter O and the numeral 0.

When the process is complete, the first task that may be asked of you is to set up your Home Group for networking. If you only have one computer, you will not have to worry about setting up a network. If you have more than one, follow the onscreen directions.

Once you have completed your installation, you can now start working with Windows 7. If you have previous computer experience, you will see all the changes from earlier versions of Windows. A great place to start learning about your new software is at the Getting Started folder. You can find that by clicking on the Start button, then in the Start Menu, Getting Started.

Windows Virtual PC

Microsoft says that all programs written for Vista, and most written for XP will work just fine in Windows 7. However, to combat the compatibility issues between Windows 7 and software designed for older versions of Windows, Microsoft developed a bit of software called Windows Virtual PC. It is a free download from Microsoft and allows you to run a Windows XP environment on your Windows 7 machine. The only real need to use this is if you are having problems with an older program working properly in Windows 7.

Sometimes the easiest solution, and the most cost and time effective, is to upgrade the program itself to a Windows 7 version. However, if that is not possible, and if you are having problems, the first step is to use Microsoft's compatibility tools. Go to:

http://windows.microsoft.com/en-us/windows7/help/compatibility

and Microsoft will help you get your programs working properly. If using all of these tools does not correct the problem, then using Virtual PC might be the answer. Go to:

http://www.microsoft.com/windows/virtual-pc to get the tools you need.

If you are an experienced Windows user, you will find that many of the tools and commands that were in plain sight in menu bars and toolbars are now hidden under icons. To see what an icon has beneath it, you can hover the pointer over it, or click the icon to see if there are more options.

But we are getting ahead of ourselves. For all the first time users of a computer, let's get back to the basics.

Product Activation

You need to activate your Windows 7 operating system whether it came on a new computer or if you upgraded from an older version of Windows. If you turn on your new computer and you are asked to activate, go ahead. You can activate either online, or via the telephone if you do not have an Internet connection. If you upgraded your computer to Windows 7, you should have activated your Windows 7 during that process. To check and see the status of your software, click on the Start button, type System in the search box, click on System in the Control Panel section of the search results, and then scroll to the bottom of the next pop up window. Your activation status will be displayed there.

Product activation verifies that you have a valid copy of Windows 7 and identifies you as the user. Once you are activated, you will have full use of Microsoft's Web sites to learn more about your computer and to keep it up to date with software improvements. This is important to keep your computer healthy and running trouble free.

Network Location

If you have a network set up in your home, or wherever you are going to use your Windows 7 computer, Windows 7 will detect it and will ask you what kind of network it is. Your choices are Home, Work or Public Networks. Windows will do the rest of the setup for you. You may need a security code for a wireless network if that is what you have established. If you have not established a network at home, but you want one, select the Home network choice and Windows will help you set up the network. A home network is a simple and effective way to share photos, files and printers among all the computers in your home.

Finalize Settings

Windows will take all of the information you gave it during the upgrade process, or when you first turned on your Windows 7 computer, and prepares your Desktop for first use.

User Account Controls

User Account Controls add a level of security to your computer. When you, or a program, make changes to your computer that should be controlled by an Administrator, a pop up box will ask you if you really want to make this change. If you do, accept the change. If you find this feature is a nuisance, you can turn it off via the Control Panel.

What Should I See On The Screen After Start-Up?

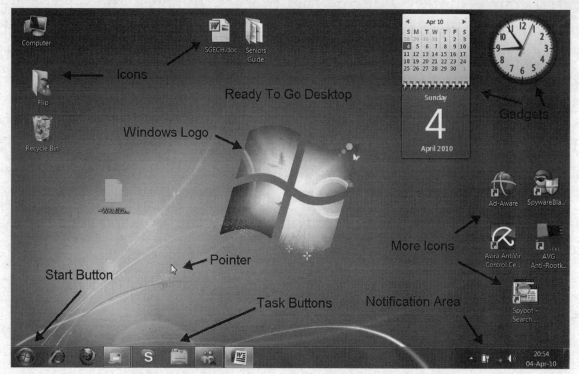

Figure 58: A Ready To Go Windows 7 Desktop

After the start-up, what you should see on the monitor is the Windows Desktop. If there are multiple users of a computer, the first screen you will see is a "user" selection screen. Each person will have their own settings for appearance, themes, choices and passwords. Select your user icon and your Desktop with your settings will appear.

The Desktop is your home base, like the physical desk where your computer sits. Several tools to get you started are placed on the background area. These include a Taskbar, icons, and a Start button. If you have a fresh installation (not upgraded from a previous version) your Windows 7 Desktop should not have any icons except the Recycle Bin.

There will be variations from computer to computer on what the Desktop looks like. You will be able to customize the look of your Desktop to suit your artistic feelings.

Anti-virus, Malware, Spyware

Every computer user needs to practice safe computing. There are a number of threats to your computer in the form of malicious software that can take control of your computer, steal data from you or even crash your computer. To practice safe computing, every computer user should use software designed to combat these problems. You should always use some form of the following programs on your computer:

Figure 59: An Arsenal of Anti-Malware Programs

- Anti-virus such as Avira Antivir, AVG Free, Symantec Norton Anti-Virus or McAfee Anti-Virus
- Anti-Spyware such as Spybot and SpyWareBlaster
- Anti-Malware such as AdAware

These are just a few of the many programs out there to help keep your computer safe. Some are free and some require subscription payments. Regardless of how much, or how little you spend on protection, you need to protect your computer.

If you have a new computer, it most likely did not come with an anti-virus program.

Windows 7 will detect that and give you a warning about using an anti-virus program. You can read this warning by clicking the little flag with a red x on it in the Notification Area of the Taskbar. Microsoft even gives you a button in the warning window that says "Find a program online". The programs listed are some of the most popular ones. Pick one from the list, or use some other anti-virus program.

Getting Started

With Vista, Microsoft had a pre-programmed Welcome Center pop up as the way to introduce you to your computer. In Windows 7, you can learn about your computer and how to make adjustments with the Getting Started feature in the Start Menu. There are tutorials that will teach you how to go onto the Internet, store photos, listen to music and much, much more.

It is also a great place to get help if you need some questions answered. Generally, every program has a help menu that you can do some research to solve any problems you are having.

To access this feature, simply click on the Start button, then on the top legend that says Getting Started. A drop down menu will give you a lot of options.

Windows Live Essentials

One of the options in Getting Started is Windows Live Essentials. In previous versions of Windows, applications to work with e-mail, photos, video etc, were included in your software package. These programs do not come with Windows 7. However, Microsoft provides all of these applications to you for free as an online download. You can get fully featured programs for e-mailing, instant messaging, organizing your photos and much, much more. Simply click

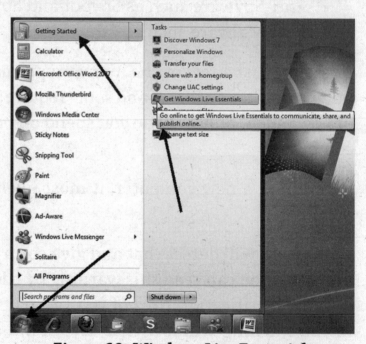

Figure 60: Windows Live Essentials

on Start, Getting Started and then click Get Windows Live Essentials. You can read about each of the programs by selecting the program name in the list. A description of the program will appear to the right of the list. Check all the programs you want, then click the Install button.

Help And Support Center

If you ever need help with a computer problem, the first place you should go is the Help and Support Center. You access that from the Start Menu. Click on Start, then in the right hand column at the bottom, click on Help and Support. You should always see if you can get your questions answered here before you call technical support. Many times you can get the help you need quicker by accessing your computer's online help references.

Switching Users

If you have more than one user account defined on your computer, several accounts can be open at the same time. You don't have to close your programs and log off to be able to switch to another user. Switching between users is easy.

- Click the Start button.
- In the bottom right corner of the Start Menu, Click the Right Arrow.
- Click Switch User. A user selection screen will pop-up.
- Select your User Name.
- Insert your password if necessary.
- Either press Enter on the keyboard or click the arrow to the right of the password. Windows 7 will come up with all of your user settings and preferences.

Basic Controls And Mechanics

The Desktop

The Desktop is the working area (background) of the Windows display on your computer.

Look at your desk at home or work. It is the area where you do your paperwork. The Desktop of a computer is where you will pull out your electronic files, write electronic letters or work in your computer-based checkbook.

When you start your computer, you will see several screens go by before you arrive at the main Windows screen, which is the Desktop. The Desktop has three main parts: Taskbar, Start Menu, and icons.

Taskbar

Figure 61: The Taskbar

The Taskbar is the horizontal bar along the bottom of the Desktop. It has the Start button on the left. Next to the Start button are the launch buttons for various programs such as Internet Explorer, Windows Explorer and Windows Media Player. Next will be the icons for open programs and windows.

The right side of the Taskbar is the notification area. Here you will see the programs or tasks that start automatically when you start Windows. On the far right, you will see the time displayed and the Aero/Show Desktop button.

The Taskbar allows you to start your navigation process through all of the computer files.

If you would like to move the Taskbar to another location, just move your cursor to the Taskbar, click and hold down the mouse button, and drag the Taskbar to another of the monitor's edges.

You can make a lot of changes to how the Taskbar works. Simply right-click on the Taskbar, select Properties from the dialog box and make all the adjustments you want to. In fact, for many facets of computing, a right-click will bring up dialog boxes that will have properties that you can adjust to enhance your computing experience.

Taskbar Buttons

The Taskbar Buttons launch programs just like clicking on a Desktop icon.

Figure 62: Taskbar Buttons

The Start button is on the left side of the Taskbar. It has the Microsoft logo on it and if you place the pointer there, the word Start will appear.

Just to the right of the Start button are the Launch Buttons. These buttons access programs you use frequently.

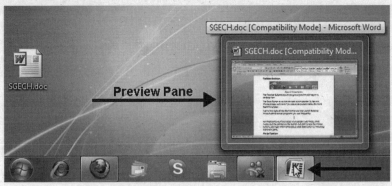

Figure 63: Taskbar Button Preview Pane

For most buttons, if you hover your pointer over them, (that means put the pointer on the button, but don't press the mouse button) you'll get information about what that button is, including a preview pane.

Pin To Taskbar

You can place any program or file icon onto the Taskbar as a way to quickly have access to them. Simply drag the icon you want to the Taskbar and release it there. Now you can quickly get to a frequently used program or file.

Taskbar Grouping

As you open programs and/or documents, the Taskbar can quickly become filled up with task buttons. To keep some semblance of order there, tasks that are using the same program will be grouped together in the Taskbar button.

Figure 64: Aero Peek Feature

For example, if you run certain virus scanning software, three or four windows might be open at any one time. Meanwhile you might want to work on a document. As the Taskbar fills up with buttons, all of the virus software windows will be grouped under one button. The document and its program will in another button. Open another document with the same program and it, too, will be grouped on the Taskbar.

To see what is in each button, simply hover the mouse pointer over a Taskbar button and the open documents will show in the Aero Peek Preview. You can select any document from the Aero Peek Preview by simply clicking on it.

Task Manager

You can keep an eye on what is going on with your computer via the Task Manager. You can see what programs and processes are running, how much of your system resources are being used, monitor performance and close programs that are not responding. Here are two ways to get to the Task Manager:

1. Simultaneously press the Ctrl, Shift, Esc keys. The Task Manager will open up.
2. Simultaneously press the Ctrl, Alt, Del keys. You will be taken to a screen that offers a number of choices. One is the Task Manager. Click that. This method is good to know if you want to log off your computer, change users or perform other tasks.

Desktop Gadgets

Windows 7 has a number of small applications for your use. These mini-apps are called Gadgets. There are hundreds of Gadgets available from calendars to day/night clocks. Want your favorite news feed displayed? You can display that too.

Figure 65: Gadgets

To add a Gadget:

- Right-click on the Desktop.
- Click Gadgets. A list will pop up of all of the available Gadgets. You can also go online to get more Gadgets.
- Select the ones that you want and drag them to the Desktop, or double-click them and they will appear on the Desktop. Initially, they will be on the right side of the Desktop but you can move them anywhere you like.

After you install a Gadget, you may be able to customize each one to make them work better for you. Hover your pointer over a Gadget and see if there is an option menu that pops up.

Start Button And Start Menu

The Start button is the button that takes you almost everywhere in Windows. It is located on the Taskbar. Clicking on the Start button brings up a single menu from which many menus and programs can be accessed.

To display the Start Menu: Click the Start button. You will see the following window:

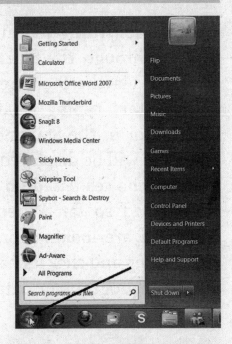

Figure 66: Start Menu

Start-Up Folder

The Start-Up folder will automatically start programs that you want running as soon as you turn on your computer. There are lots of programs that start when you turn on the computer, but this folder allows you to customize what you want.

For example, if you want the calculator turned on every time you start your computer, just follow these steps:

- Find the program you want, for our example, the calculator.
- Right-click on it and create a shortcut on the Desktop.
- Click the Start button.
- Select All Programs.
- Select Start-Up or right-click Open,
- Drag the shortcut you created to the Start-Up folder.

Almost everything you might want to find through the Start Menu is available via the Start Search box. Simply start typing what you are looking for in the Start Search Box and a list will be displayed of all the possible choices based on what you have typed so far. When you see what you are looking for, you can stop typing and click its name in the list. That program, or data file, will open.

Figure 67: Start Search Box Before Typing

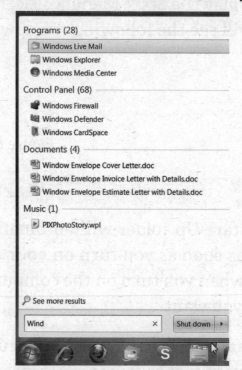

Figure 68: Search Box And List
After Starting To Type

Pinning To The Start Menu

Just like you can pin programs and files to the Taskbar, you can also pin items to the Start Menu. The Start Menu displays a list of programs that you have recently used. This list will change as your computer history grows. If you would like some programs to show up at the top of the Start Menu all the time, you can pin them to the Start Menu. A line will be drawn dividing the start menu into a top section and bottom section once you have pinned something to the Start Menu. The top section is for the items pinned to the Start Menu and will always stay there until you unpin them. The bottom section is for recently used programs. These will change based on your usage.

To pin a program to the Start Menu:

- Right-click on the program.
- Select Pin To Start Menu. The program icon will shift to the upper section.

To unpin a selection:

- Right-click on a program in the pinned area.
- Select Unpin From Start Menu. The icon will leave the upper section.

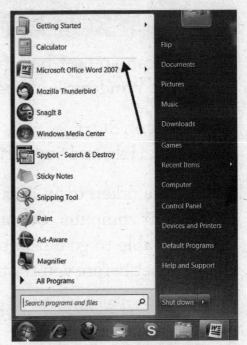

Figure 69: Dividing Line For Pinned Items

Recent Items

Recent Items are files you have been working with lately. They might be individual letters, photos, documents, etc. Via the Start Menu, you can quickly see a list of those Recent Items and open them.

To see that list:

- Click on Start.
- Type Recent in the Search Box.
- Pick the type of Recent items you want to look at.

If you want an easy way to see your recent documents, rather than have to search every time, Click the Start button, then right-click in a blank area of the Start Menu box. Select Properties and scroll down the list to Recent and check the box. Now Recent Items will display on the ride side of the Start Menu. Clicking Recent Items will bring up a list of your recently looked at items. Then click on the item you want and it will open.

Help And Support System

Not only can you get help from The Getting Started selection on the Start Menu, but Windows 7 offers lots of help via the Help and Support Menu.

- Click on Start.
- Click Help and Support.

You will be taken to an area where you can find out information about how to use your computer, or solve a problem. Some of the help features require you to be able to go out onto the Internet. Make sure you are connected to the Internet before you try to find support out there.

Search Help

Search Help is a tool to quickly find the information you need to solve a problem.

- After you click Help and Support, a window appears and at the top is a rectangular typing box with "Search Help" in it.
- Place your cursor there and type a topic you want to get help with.
- Press Enter on your keyboard.
- A list of possible solutions/answers to your question will appear in a new window. Click on one of the topics and you will be able to read about that topic.

Keep in mind that the computer help function cannot read minds. You may have to modify your request a bit until you get the information you are looking for.

Guided Help

Once you ask for help, you may get more than just information. You may get the steps to solve your issue. Simply click on the links as they come up (words highlighted in blue) and follow the instructions.

Sometimes, you are offered an automatic solution to your problem. The computer will try to fix the issue for you. For the most part, these automatic fixes work great. During this process, you may be asked questions pertaining to your issue. Once again, the computer is not a mind reader. It is just looking for information from you so it can apply the best solution.

Shutting Down

There are two ways to shut down your computer. You can put it to sleep, or you can completely power it down. To completely Shut Down your computer with a complete power-off:

- Select Start.
- Click on the button on the lower right that says Shutdown.

To put your computer to sleep:

- Click the Start button.
- Click the little arrow just to the right of the Shutdown button. Select Sleep. Your work is saved, the display turns off and the computer goes into sleep mode. This allows you to quickly resume work when you get back to your computer.

To wake your computer, just slightly press the power button.

Frozen Computer

Every once in a while your PC may experience a puzzling failure. It may just freeze up for no reason at all. **DO NOT WORRY. YOU DID NOT DO IT!** It is just the nature of computers to get confused on occasion. When this happens, your mouse will stop responding, the keyboard is not functional and the computer just sits and stares at you. That pesky machine just won't respond to your inputs. You will need to restart the computer.

First, try to shutdown the frozen program:

- Click the Close [X] button in the upper right-hand corner of the window.
- If that does not work, press these three keys at the same time: Ctrl, Alt, Del. Select Task Manager from the list.
- Under the Applications tab, find the frozen program in the list, a notation may say "Program Not Responding". Select it and click End Program.

- If that did not work, Click the Start button.
- Click the lower right arrow, then Restart.
- If that did not work, an alternate method is to press and hold the Ctrl and Alt keys, then press the Del key three times.
- If that did not work, here's the last ditch method. Turn off the power button on the computer. Let it rest for a minute or so and then turn it back on. On a number of computers, you must hold in the power button until the computer shuts down.

Restarting Your Computer

One reason to restart a computer is if you have loaded a new program. Sometimes Windows requires a restart for all the new settings to take effect. In this case, just use the Start Menu Restart procedure. Sometimes, the new program will offer to restart the computer for you.

Moving A Window

You may want to rearrange where a window is located on your Desktop. Follow these steps to move a window:

- Place the pointer on the window's title bar.
- Drag the title bar to the location you want and release the mouse button.

This will not work if your window is in full screen mode. Full screen means this one window takes up all the space on your monitor. You need to reduce the size of the window in order to be able to move it around.

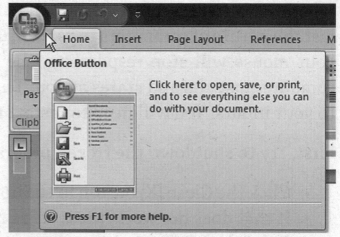

Figure 70: Microsoft Logo "File" Button

In many Microsoft programs, rather than File being displayed in the upper left toolbar, a Microsoft logo is displayed. Many functions that we used to find under File will be found there.

Switching Between Windows

To look at a window that is not on top of the stack:

- Click on the window you want.
- Click on its Taskbar button.
- A new feature of Windows 7 is the Aero Peek Button just to the right of the Notification Area. Clicking the Aero Button allows you to easily see how many windows are open on the Desktop, get back to the Desktop rapidly and manage all your windows. It's a pretty cool shortcut to help you keep organized while you are working.
- When you select the window by any of these methods, the window will jump to the top of the stack.

Too Many Open Windows?

There are some commands you can use to "clean-up" the window clutter on your Desktop. If you have too many open windows:

- Right-click the mouse anywhere on the Taskbar and a menu appears.
- Select Cascade Windows. The Cascade command displays the windows so that the title bar of each window appears.
- Click on any title bar to bring its window to the front of each stack.
- Show Windows Stacked displays each window in horizontal panes and the Show Windows Side by Side displays each window in vertical panes.
- Click the Aero Quick Launch button to stack the windows for easy viewing.

You should always close a window once you are finished working with it. This will really help tame Desktop clutter.

Aero Snaps

Aero Snaps is a new feature of Windows 7. It allows you to quickly re-size a window. If you want to maximize a window, put your pointer on the Title Bar, and drag the window to the top of your screen. When the pointer gets to the top of the screen, the window will snap to full screen mode. If you drag the pointer and window to the left side of the screen, the window will snap to half size on the left side of the screen. If you drag it to the right, it will occupy the right side of the screen at half size. This is a great way to have two documents side by side.

Windows Flip And Flip 3D

Another way to keep track of your open windows and to switch between them is through Windows Flip and Flip 3D. To use Windows Flip, press the Alt key, and then Tab, and cycle through the open windows by continuing to press Tab. You will see each window as a miniature version of itself in a film strip. When you release the Alt button, the preview you are looking at will become the active window.

To use Flip 3D, which is similar to Windows Aero in Vista, click the Windows key and Tab. You will see a larger version of the preview of each open window. Each time you press the Tab key the windows will cycle so you can see what is open. Again, release the Windows key when you want a preview to become the active window.

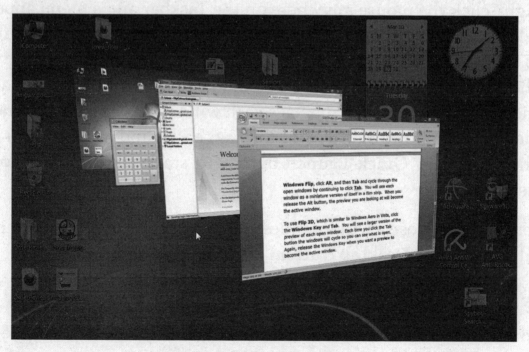

Figure 71: Windows Flip 3D

Using Menus And Sub-Menus

It is as simple as this:

- On the menu bar, choose the category of the command that you want. The menu opens.
- Click on the command you want.

If a sub-menu opens, it is just giving you more options of how to accomplish your task at hand. Find what you want and once again click on it.

Shortcut Menus

A shortcut menu or alternate menu is a hidden menu that can be shown with a right-click of the mouse. Almost every object on your computer has one. These are frequently used commands that are made easy to get to with one right-click.

The commands vary from program to program so you should right-click in every program you use to get an idea of what commands are at "your fingertips".

Windows 7 Tasks

Finding Files And Folders

When you are looking for a particular folder or file, and you are not sure where it is located on your computer, you can use the Search command instead of opening numerous folders. The Search command lets you quickly search a specific drive or your entire computer.

To find a file or folder:

- Click the Start button, click in the box that says Search programs and files.
- Start to type the file or folder name you want to find.

The results will start appearing in the Start Window. The more you type, the narrower the results will be.

If you know that you are looking for a particular type of file or folder, for example a document, instead of using the Start button search, open the documents folder itself, and type your request in the search box in the upper right corner. Now the search will be conducted just in documents.

A word to the wise: start filing your information in an orderly manner at the beginning of your computer experience. It will make life easier!

Opening A File Or Folder

After you have located the file you want, either through a search or by going straight to it in a directory, you can double-click on it to open it.

To find and open a file or folder without using Search:

- On the Desktop, double-click Computer.
- Double-click the drive that contains the file or folder you want to open.
- Double-click the file or folder.

If you have recently opened a file that you want to look at again, check Recent Items in the Start Menu. You can also open files and folders from the File Open command in the application itself. For example, if you are working in Microsoft Word, you can find other Word created documents by using the File Open method. A list of your Word documents will show up.

Creating A File Or Folder

To create a folder:

- On the Desktop, double-click Computer.
- Double-click the disk drive or folder in which you want to create a folder. The drive or folder opens.
- On the Menu Bar, click New Folder.

An alternate way is to:

- Right-click a blank area on the Desktop.
- Click New.
- Click Folder and it will appear.

- While the "New Folder" title is highlighted, type a folder name of your choice and then press Enter.
- If you do not want the new folder to reside on the Desktop, drag it to the location you want it to move to.

Naming A File Or Folder

If you're saving something for the first time, Windows 7 asks you to name the file or document. Type something descriptive. Use only letters, numbers, and spaces between the words. You can't use any of the following characters: : / \ * | < > ? "

The last three letters (suffix) of a file name designate an extension. An extension identifies the format of the file. It is preceded by a period. Every file is in a specific format. There are many different formats.

By naming a file with an extension, you tell the computer which format the file is in. That way the computer knows what format to use each time you want to work with that file. Most programs automatically add the extension suffix when you save your work. For example, Microsoft Word documents end with the file extension .doc or .docx while Microsoft Excel spreadsheets end with the extension .xls.

Renaming A File Or Folder

It is simple to rename a file or folder. To rename:

- Select the file or folder you want to rename. On the Organize menu, click Rename.
- Type a name and press Enter.

Or

- Select the file or folder you want to rename.
- Right-click on it and select Rename from the shortcut menu.
- Type a name and press Enter.

Be careful about renaming your files without thinking about it first. Shortcuts that use an old file name will no longer work. If you have linked a file to a program with an old name, the link will no longer work either.

File conflicts exist when you try to name two different files with the same name. If you are creating the second file, Windows 7 will warn you when you try to save a file name that already exists. Windows 7 will offer three possible solutions:

- Replace Existing File.
- Save Changes with a Different Name.
- Merge Changes Into Existing File.

Make sure you read the selections and pick the one that is most appropriate for what you want.

You should normally name each file with separate, specific names. For example, a lettertoson.docx should not be used for every letter to your son. The next letter could be lettertoson2.docx, lettertoson3.docx etc. If you make a copy of the file named lettertoson.docx, the copy will be titled lettertoson. docx (copy1). That way you can have this one letter appear as different files.

Copying Or Moving A File Or Folder

There are two simple ways to copy or move files and folders. To copy a file or folder:

- Right-click on a file or folder.
- Select Copy.
- Go to where you want the copy to appear and right-click.
- Select Paste. A copy of the original folder will appear.

To move a file or folder:

- Right-click the file or folder.
- Click Send To.
- Select from the list of likely locations.

You can also move a file by dragging its icon from one location to another:

- Open the folder that holds your file or folder that you want to move.
- Also open the destination folder.
- Re-size both windows so they both appear on your Desktop.
- Click on the target file or folder, hold down the mouse button and drag it to the destination folder. The icon will disappear from the original folder and appear in the new folder.

Folder Options

You can change how you see your folders just as you can modify your Desktop. You get choices everywhere with Windows 7!

- Open a folder.
- Click on Organize. From the drop down menu, click Folder and Search Options. From here you can make adjustments to how your folders look and act.

One recommendation is to click on Show Hidden Files, Folders and Drives. You never know when you are going to need to find something that is normally hidden. It's a good idea to be set up for it now. Un-checking Hide Extensions For Known File Types also helps you to see exactly what extensions are being used for every file.

Viewing Folders

There are a number of ways to look at each and every document, file or folder. You control this with the View Menu. For example, you might want your photos in a large icon format. This will give you a preview of each of your photos while still in the folder view. For documents, you may want a title list instead. You can choose your views for each and every folder from the View menu.

To change how you view inside any folder:

- Click on the Change Your View icon on the menu bar. This icon is the third from the right, and if you hover your pointer on it, it will say Change Your View.
- Adjust the settings as necessary.

Customizing Folders

You can "dress up" your folders by adding a picture or icon to any folder.

- Simply find a folder you want to customize.
- Right-click on a blank spot of the folder.
- Click Properties, then the Customize tab. A dialog box will appear so you can browse your computer and place a picture on the folder cover or change its icon.

Once again, you'll need to play around a bit to get used to "massaging" your computer to the way you want it.

Compressed Folders

Compressed folders hold files that have been reduced in size so they take up less room on your disks. They are known as "zipped" folders and have a little zipper on the icon. These folders have not lost any important information from your files, but through some "propeller head" technology, they've squeezed the files down in size as you would a sponge.

Most users do not need to compress files and folders. However, if you find you need to, read on.

To compress files:

- Create a new compressed folder by right-clicking on an empty area of the Desktop.
- Click New Compressed (zipped) Folder. A new folder will appear.
- Name this new folder.
- Drag your files that you want to compress to this new folder. Now they're compressed.

To get them back from being compressed, just drag them to a non-compressed folder and they will come back. However, a compressed copy will remain in the compressed folder.

If someone sends you a compressed file, simply drag it out of the compressed folder and it will "reconstitute" itself. Again, most folks will not need to compress files.

Sorting Folders

While working in Windows 7, you can sort folders in a number of different ways. By looking at the header bar, you will see various criteria that Windows can sort by. Want to see the folder list of when you last worked in the folders?

- Click the Date header in the document list and the order will change.

Want a reverse alphabetical listing?

- Click the Name header in the document list. Or,
- Click the little arrow to change from ascending to descending (or back).

You can also right-click to get to a Sort by command and quickly sort in a number of different ways.

Grouping Folders

You can arrange the contents of a folder in groups. For example, if you want all of the contents of a folder displayed by type, you can then have a list that shows all of the sub-folders in a grouping, all the Microsoft Word documents in a grouping, etc.

To set up groups, right-click on an empty section of a folder, then click on Sort by. Choose your criteria, or look for other criteria in the More section.

Deleting A File Or Folder

To delete a file or folder:

- Right-click on the icon.
- Select Delete. This will send the file or folder to the Recycle Bin. Alternately, you can click on the icon and drag it to the Recycle Bin.

Customizing The Desktop

You can change the appearance to suit your desires. You can move icons around, remove icons, add icons, change the colors and so much more.

If you don't like the standard color scheme on your Desktop, you can change it. You can use pre-defined color schemes or make up your own. If your color selections are too wild they may cause eye strain!

- Right-click on an empty portion of the Desktop.
- A pop-up menu appears. Click on Personalize and you will be given a number of tabs to make changes.

Some folks worry that they'll make a change that "ruins" their computer. Don't worry. Play around a bit. You can always put things back the way they were.

Arranging Icons On The Desktop

You can arrange your icons any way you want.

- Put your pointer on each icon you want to move.
- Click and hold down the left mouse button and drag the icons where you want them. Then release the button.
- Right-click on a blank spot on the Desktop.
- Select View and then un-check Auto Arrange and Align to Grid. Your icons should stay put.
- By clicking Auto Arrange, the computer will put them where it thinks they should go. With Align to Grid, they will be stacked neatly on the Desktop.

I like to put my anti-virus icons on the right side to remind me to run my scans. I keep the documents that I am working on in the middle of the Desktop. I keep the Computer, Recycle Bin and other frequently used icons on the left side.

Playing A CD

Playing music with the CD Player is very simple. A feature called auto-play detects when you insert a CD into the CD drive and automatically starts the music for you.

If auto-play does not work, here is how to do it manually:

- Click the Start button.
- Select All Programs.
- Select Windows Media Player.
- Select the CD title in the list on the left.
- Select the song title in the right pane.

Another method is to double click the Computer icon. Then double click the drive you inserted the CD in. When you click a track, your default media player will play the music.

You do not have to use Windows Media Player. If you have a different player on your computer, follow their instructions for their product. Other players include iTunes, Real Player and Adobe Media Player, just to name a few.

Playing Media Clips And Movies

Playing any media format is easy with Windows Media Player.

- Open the player as you did on the previous page by going to Start.
- Click All Programs.
- Click Windows Media Player (or click the Windows Media Player icon).
- On the File menu, click Open.
- Browse and locate the file you want to view or hear.
- Click on that and it should start playing.

If you receive a media file via e-mail, it probably played just fine when you clicked on it. However, if you try to find it while it is still in your e-mail inbox via a media player, you might not find it. If this happens: save the media file to a folder outside of your e-mail program.

Windows Media Center

This is a more advanced version of Windows Media Player. Not only can you play CDs and DVDs, but Windows Media Center will catalog all digital media content on your computer to give you a one-stop viewing location for videos, movies, photos and much more. In addition, with the correct hardware added, you can listen to FM radio broadcasts and even watch TV on your computer monitor. When you first start Windows Media Center, you will need to run a setup program. Express Setup works best for most users.

Screen Saver

A screen saver is a program that displays an image or animation on your screen when your PC is idle.

It was invented to insure that all parts of the monitor screen received equal amounts of illumination so a ghost image would not be "burned" onto the screen. Today's monitors don't have burn-in problems and screen savers are not really necessary, but almost everyone uses them anyway.

Screen savers are fun and often entertaining. You can use any number of pre-installed screen savers or you can use screen savers downloaded from the Internet. You can even use any of your saved digital photos.

Windows 7 comes with some screen savers as part of the package. There are many more screen savers available commercially. To find the screen savers included with Windows 7:

- Right-click on a blank spot on the Desktop.
- Select Personalize to open the display properties dialog box.
- Click the Screen Saver link in the bottom right corner
- Select an option from the drop-down list.
- Make adjusts to the timing to suit your desires.
- Click OK to make this your screen saver.

To use images you have stored on your computer as your screen saver, simply pick Photos as your screen saver option.

Burn To Disc

To burn a disc simply means to make a copy. You could be copying music from your computer to a CD so you can play some tunes in your car. You could also be backing up your checkbook files. This is also known as burning. The term is used whether you are copying to a CD or DVD.

Windows 7 makes it easy to burn files.

- First, make sure you have the correct discs for the type of drive you have. You cannot burn a DVD in a CD drive.
- Select the file you want to copy.
- Click on the Burn button on the menu bar. Follow the instructions.

Recycle Bin

The Recycle Bin is just another folder that holds the files and folders you want to permanently delete. However, just like the trash at home, you have to "take it out" to really get rid of them.

Until you empty the Recycle Bin, the files and folders can be moved back to wherever you want them. This way you do not have to worry about sending things to the Recycle Bin and then wondering if you should not have thrown them out.

When you delete files and folders from your hard disk drive they are moved to the Recycle Bin. However, files and folders that you delete from the command prompt don't go into the Recycle Bin. For example, if you start working on a document and don't save it, and then you close the window, your work will not be saved and it will not appear in the Recycle Bin.

To get something out of the Recycle Bin:

- Click on the Recycle Bin icon.
- Either click on Restore All in the menu bar to return everything back to your computer or,
- Right-click on an individual file or folder and select Restore. The file or folder will be restored to your Desktop.

Program Compatibility

As we mentioned earlier, some programs written for earlier versions of Windows may not run well, or at all, in Windows 7. If you come across this issue with one of your programs, Microsoft has given you a tool to try and resolve the issue. It is called The Windows Program Compatibility Troubleshooter. To get to this tool:

- Click on Start, Control Panel and then System.
- Click Action Center in the lower left corner.
- Then click Windows Program Compatibility Troubleshooter.

Program Buttons

Program Buttons appear on the Taskbar to identify any open applications or programs currently being used along with the documents you are working on. On the right side of the Taskbar you will see programs that start automatically when you start Windows.

If a program is minimized (meaning it does not appear on the screen, but is still running), clicking on it from the Taskbar brings it back on-screen. You can easily switch to a different window by clicking its program button on the Taskbar.

Removing A Program

The best way to uninstall a program is by using the Programs and Features icon, located in the Control Panel.

It is not a good idea to simply delete the program folder from the Computer Icon or Windows Explorer. The original program installation may have put files in other folders and changed some of the system settings.

To remove a program:

- Click the Start and then Control Panel.
- Double-click the Programs and Features icon.
- Select the program you want to uninstall.
- Select Uninstall. There are two other options in this dialog box: Change or Repair. You will rarely use them.

Windows Explorer

Windows Explorer is a method of seeing everything on your computer. You look at the contents through a single window in a hierarchical structure.

The left side of the Windows Explorer window contains a list of your drives and folders, and the right side displays the contents of any folder you select from the left side list. You can use the Change View icon in the menu bar to change how the icons on the right half of the window appear. To use Windows Explorer:

- Click the Windows Explorer icon on the Taskbar.
- In the left pane, click the letter that represents your hard drive. The hard drive contents will appear in the right pane.
- To see a preview of each folder you are looking at, click the icon just to the left of the Get Help question mark in the menu bar. This icon adjusts how the preview pane works.

Windows Explorer is more than just a filing structure. It is the management tool that keeps your computer in good running order. Windows Explorer manages the Taskbar groupings and allows you to hover your mouse over icons and buttons to see what is there.

Looking At Folders Inside Windows Explorer

When you start working with Windows Explorer, you will be looking at folders. When you click on a folder, you will be looking at the folders inside that folder. You continue to look down into the filing structure until you find the file you want to work with. This might be a document, a photo or a music file. To the computer, they are all the same: just files.

Once you find the file you are looking for, you can easily see where it is located by looking at the Address Bar.

Computer Folder

The Computer Folder is another way to view the entire contents of your computer. It allows you to browse drives, directories (folders) and files.

Figure 72: Computer Icon

Unlike Windows Explorer which shows you the contents in a hierarchical structure, clicking on the Computer Icon shows you the contents of a single folder or drive.

For example, if you click on the Computer Icon either on the Desktop or in the Start Menu, you will see the next level of folders and files that are stored there. That level includes your hard drive, your removable drives and maybe a few folders. Obviously your computer holds more than that.

Click on the hard drive and now you see the contents of the hard drive. Keep working through your drive until you find the folder or file you want.

Exploring My Drives

It does not matter whether you look through your drives with Windows Explorer or My Computer. You will get the same results. However, you will gravitate to the method you like best.

The reason you may want to look through the drives is to see the entire contents of a drive, find lost folders or documents, or move files around. There is a lot you can accomplish by looking through the filing architecture of your computer.

Differences Between Drives

All drives that are attached to a computer are assigned a letter. It's a simple way to tell them apart. The designations are A:, B:, C:, D:, E:, F: etc. As you add more peripheral drives, your computer will automatically assign them a letter.

In the past, the A: drive was for the floppy drive. The B: drive was for a second floppy. The C: drive was the computer's main hard drive. Even though your computer may not have any floppies, by convention, most computers' hard drives are the C: drive. If your computer came with a second installed hard drive, or partitioned your only hard drive into two parts, the second hard drive or part will be the D: drive.

You can see all the drives connected to your computer by clicking on the Computer icon.

Navigation Pane

The Navigation Pane is on the left side of the Windows Explorer or Computer Folder. You can find any file or folder by working your way through the Navigation Pane and seeing the results in the window to the right. If a legend in the Navigation Pane has a little arrowhead by it that means there are more items within that legend. Click that arrowhead to see more.

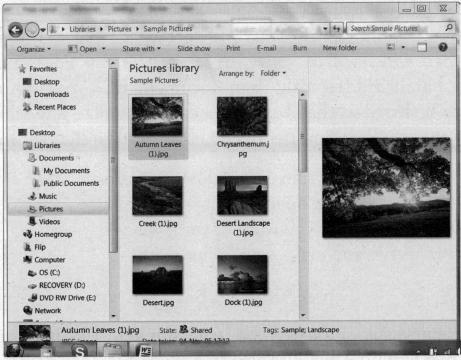

Figure 73: Navigation Pane

Libraries

The Library is Windows 7's way of organizing your files. What used to be known as Documents, Music, Pictures and Videos in Vista, are now organized into Libraries. Within each Library, there is a private and public folder.

So for example, in the Documents Library, there will be a folder for My Documents and a folder for Public Documents.

You can create other Libraries as you need them. They can be sub-folders of current Libraries, or you can create new Libraries. The Library is simply a way of organizing what is stored on your computer.

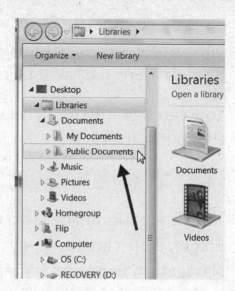

Figure 74: Public and My Documents Folders

Customizing The Library

When you first create a Library, you can select what kinds of files you will be cataloging there which will optimize the Library for you. For example, music files will be handled differently than document files. You can also select other files to be listed in the library. You can customize any Library file at any time by going to its Properties dialog box. To make changes to a Library:

- Click on the Computer icon or Windows Explorer.
- In the Navigation Pane, open the Libraries icon.
- Right-click the Library you want to work with.
- Select Properties and make your adjustments.

Address Bar

The Address Bar displays the location "trail" for your file. It shows the file's location in hierarchal format all the way back to the hard drive. But it also allows you to jump to any of the locations displayed in the address bar. In the following picture, if you clicked on Documents, you would be shown a list of files in the Documents Folder. Click on one of those, and you will go there.

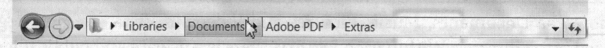

Figure 75: Navigation Pane Address Bar

Undo

Word processors have had an Undo command for quite some time. Computers remember the steps they take as you do your work. By clicking Undo from the Edit Menu, you can back track through your document to fix errors, remove formatting changes or just to get back to a previous state of the document.

Windows 7 adds that functionality to your folders. If you change the name of a folder, but decide to change it back, simply right-click that folder and select Undo. If you deleted a folder, you can get it back through the same process by right-clicking on the folder that held the soon to be restored deleted folder.

Recent Items

Windows 7 keeps track of the items you have recently been working on. Through the use of Jump Lists, each program from the Start Menu can show you what you have been working on recently. Click on Start, then hover the pointer on a program in the Start Menu list that has a small arrow on it. A list will open of the recently worked on items. Click an item and it will open.

Previous Windows users will notice that the Recent Items option on the right side of the Start Menu is gone. Since each program has a jump list, you can see program specific recent items, rather than all of the recent items lumped together. However, you can get your Recent Items list back by right-clicking on the Start button, click Properties, select the Start Menu tab and then click the Customize button. Scroll down and place a check mark in the Recent Items selection. You will now have the Recent Items back on the Start Menu.

Resource Monitor

If you ever want to 'look under the hood' and see what is going on deep inside your computer, use the Resource Monitor. You access this handy trouble-shooting tool by clicking on Start, All Programs, Accessories, System Tools and then Resource Monitor. There is all sorts of propeller head information here. One day though, you may need to troubleshoot an issue with your computer so now you know where to find this valuable resource.

Maintenance

Your computer will run trouble free if you just do some basic housekeeping steps. Check the section on the Action Center to see how easy it is to keep up to speed on your housekeeping tasks.

- Use an anti-virus program and anti-malware programs and update them regularly.
- Keep your Windows 7 program up to date with Microsoft's Windows Update features.
- Run Disk Cleanup regularly.
- Run Disk Defragmentation periodically.
- Dust your monitor and keyboard.
- Do not use chemical cleaners. If a bit of cleaning is needed, use just a little water: a damp sponge.
- Keep all vents clear of obstructions.

System Properties

Want to find out more about your computer details? You can check your system properties at any time.

- Right-click the Computer icon on your Desktop.
- Click Properties. You will get a box chock full of information about your computer.

There are other ways of finding this same information. You can go to the Control Panel and click on System. You might need to find this page if you are working with tech support people to solve a problem.

Performance Information

Microsoft gives you tools to see how well your computer is performing against the 'benchmark' Windows system. To see how well your computer is performing:

- Open the System Properties box as described above.
- Click Performance Information and Tools in the lower left corner of the box.

A new screen will open showing you various scores for system components. This is a relative scoring system and you do not need to pay much attention to it unless you are unhappy with your computer's overall performance.

From this page, you can find out information on how to improve performance in various areas. Sometimes it just requires a little housekeeping. Other solutions require spending money. Unless you absolutely have to, don't spend extra money for computer improvements that may not give you much more performance.

Disk Clean Up

Disk Clean Up is a utility function that removes unnecessary files from your computer. This should be considered a good housekeeping tool and should be done frequently. This will help keep your performance high.

To run Disk Clean Up:

- Go to the Performance section.
- Right-click on Computer.
- Click Properties, click Performance Information and Tools.
- In the left menu, click Open Disk Clean Up.
- Select the drive you want to clean and click on OK. (It may take a few minutes to discover all that can be deleted.)
- When shown the results, make sure all the boxes are checked.
- Click OK. All the files will be permanently deleted.

Defragging

Computers store information in clusters. However, the clusters of one file may not all be stored in the same area of the hard drive. This is normal and over time, the hard drive's ability to retrieve these clusters slows down as more and more clusters are farther and farther apart. When this happens, the disk is fragmented.

To improve performance, you can straighten up the disk and put the files back in order. This is known as defragging.

To defrag your disk:

- Click Start.
- Type in the search box Disk Defrag or just Defrag.
- Click Disk Defragmenter. The Disk Defragmenter dialog box will open up.
- To defrag right now, click the Defragment Now button.

You will notice an area of this box that allows you to schedule Defrags for the future. See the next topic for more information.

Scheduling Maintenance Tasks

While in the Defrag box, you can set up a schedule for future defrags. Choose a time when no one is using the computer and the computer will be on. I usually use one or two o'clock in the morning. Yes, that means I leave my computer on overnight.

To set up future defrags:

- Click the Configure Schedule button in the Disk Defragmenter box. Adjust the time and dates.
- Click OK.

To schedule other tasks, including maintenance tasks:

- Click Start.
- Type in the Search Box "Task Scheduler".
- Click Task Scheduler in the Start list. Follow the instructions within the boxes.

There are many things you can schedule with Task Scheduler. You can even remind yourself to take your daily vitamins!

Backing Up

The best back-up method is the one that you do! I'm not trying to be flippant; backing up is important. If you back up irregularly, you are at risk of losing the information stored on your computer. If the information is not important to you, or is easily replaced from paper files, then you do not have to worry about backing up. However, most of us need the information on our computers. Daily!

I like backing up to an external hard drive. However, not everyone has one. Backing up your files to disk is fairly easy.

- Click on Start.
- Type in the Search Box "Backup".
- Click Backup and Restore from either the top of the list or from the Control Panel section.
- If this is your first time backing up, you will have to click on Set up Backup. Follow the instruction.

If you are using CD or DVD discs, make sure you have the appropriate kind for your drive, and plenty of them.

Follow the on-screen directions pertaining to drive selection and start times.

Recovery

If your computer ever crashes, and you need to recover your files, you will be very thankful you kept your backups up to speed. Once you have an operating system working again, you can restore your files through the Backup and Restore folder in the Control Panel. Select the Restore function on the bottom of the list in this folder.

System Restore

Every once in awhile, when you install some program that you think is going to make your computing experience better, your computer becomes erratic and stops functioning properly. The program just is not compatible with your operating system. Generally, removing the program and all its drivers solves the issue. However, sometimes this does not work. In that case, we can take the computer 'back in time' and restore your system settings to a date before you installed the offending program.

Windows 7 creates a Restore Point every time you install a new program, and once a week just for good measure. You can manually create a Restore Point whenever you feel like it.

To create, or make use of a System Restore Point:

- Right-click the Computer icon.
- Click Properties.
- In the left actions list, select Advanced system settings.
- Then select the System Protection tab.
- At the bottom of the box is a Create button. Click to Create a Restore Point.
- At the top of the box is a System Restore button. Click that to start the Restore process.

If you are restoring to a time before an instability was created, make sure you pick a restore point before the offending program was added.

Windows Firewall

A firewall keeps intruders out of your computer. You should always have one turned on. Windows 7 has its own firewall and you should use it if you do not have another one. If you have another firewall that you want to use, great! Install it and turn it on. However, you should turn the Windows 7 firewall off. Two firewalls running at the same time will not work well together.

To check on your Windows Firewall:

- Click on Start, then the Control Panel.
- Click Windows Firewall to change settings.
- Turn it on or off, or to allow exceptions to get through the firewall. The exceptions tab is rarely used for most home users so you should not have to deal with this.

Malware Protection

Malware harms your computer. Malware is defined as malicious software. It is software that you do not want on your computer. It generally comes via e-mail that you download onto your computer.

Malware is further delineated as spyware, adware, viruses, Trojans and any number of other nomenclature designations that will be created in the future.

Windows Defender is Windows 7's weapon against spyware and adware. It is automatically turned on when you turn on your computer. Windows Defender scans your computer for malware infections. By default, Windows Defender scans your computer at 2 AM. This is a good reason to keep your computer on overnight. However, from the Tools menu in Windows Defender, you can adjust the scan time to suit your schedule.

In the left hand section of the window are some links. Change Settings is where you can customize how Windows Update works. You can elect not to update (NOT RECOMMENDED!), inform you of updates and allow you to select the ones you want, or update automatically and at what time, and how often.

Windows Update Feature

Windows Update is a service provided by Microsoft to keep your computer in tip top condition, software wise. It will install updates to Windows and other Microsoft programs, patches for problems that arise in Microsoft programs and help keep your computer secure and performing well.

You can elect to let Microsoft update your computer automatically, or just inform you that updates are available. At The Senior's Guide, we recommend that you use the automatic feature. This means once again you should leave your computer on when you schedule Windows to update.

To check your settings in Windows Update:

- Simply click Start, then Control Panel.
- Click Windows Update.

- The main window tells you the status of Windows Update. If this is your first time going to Windows Update, you should update your computer right away.

Action Center

The Action Center is a centralized hub to take care of Security and Maintenance issues. Although we've shown you how to get to various parts of your computer in their individual pathways, i.e. Performance Indicators, Windows Update, etc, the Action Center groups all of these functions in one easy to use place. Want to work with Backup and Restore? Here it is. So is Windows Update, Windows Troubleshooting and so much more. Windows 7 even puts an icon in your system tray to alert you to any issues that may need attention.

101 Windows 7 Tips And Tricks

1. You can "dock" a window to the left or right half of the screen by simply dragging it to the edge.

2. You can drag the window to the top of the screen to maximize it, and double-click the window top / bottom border to maximize it vertically with the same horizontal width.

3. To minimize all the non-active background windows, press the Windows + Home keys.

4. There are several sets of themed wallpapers installed based on the language you choose, but the others are in a hidden directory. Just double-click on the theme file in the Theme directory to display a rotation through all the pictures for that country.

5. You can right-click the Title bar area or left-click the Control icon, to display the Control menu.

6. The icons in the Taskbar aren't fixed in-place. You can reorder them whether they're pinned shortcuts or running applications. Drag the system tray icons around to rearrange their order, or move them in and out of the hidden icon list. It's an easy way to customize your system to show the things you want, where you want them.

7. To achieve the Vista style Taskbar-look, right-click on the Taskbar and choose the properties dialog. Select the "small icons" checkbox and under the

"Taskbar buttons" setting, choose "combine when Taskbar is full".

8. The Aero Peek feature is not available in the Starter or Home Basic editions of Windows 7.

9. Press Ctrl+T to open a new tab in Internet Explorer. If you want to keep one tab open and close all others, right-click the tab you want to keep open and choose Close Other Tabs.

10. If you've already got an application open on your Desktop and you want to open a second instance of the same application, you don't have to go back to the start menu. Hold down the Shift key while clicking on the Taskbar icon, and it will open a new instance of the application rather than switching to the existing application.

11. You can choose the color and size of mouse pointers in the Make the Mouse Easier to Use dialog box.

12. If you forget your password and try to switch users without entering one, Windows shows your password hint, which you can set when you initially choose your password.

13. If you're always working in the same four or five folders, you can quickly pin them with the Explorer icon on the Taskbar. Hold the right-click button down and drag the folder to the Taskbar, and it will be automatically pinned in the Explorer Jump List.

14. Whenever you see "Press Any Key", remember that you can press any key you choose: X, Y, and Z, the Spacebar, whatever you like. There is not an "Any" key.

15. Windows 7 doesn't include a movie editing tool.

16. Windows 7 now includes the ability to create a system repair disc, which is essentially a CD-bootable version of Windows that just includes the command prompt and a suite of system tools. Just type "system repair disc" in the Start Menu search box, and you'll be led to the utility.

17. Pressing the Windows and plus or minus keys activates the Magnifier, which lets you zoom in on the entire Desktop or open a rectangular magnifying lens to zoom in and out of parts of your screen. You can customize the Magnifier options to follow your mouse pointer or keyboard cursor. The Magnifier only works when Aero Desktop is enabled.

18. If a window is not maximized, pressing Windows + Page Up will fill it to your screen. Windows + Page Down will minimize that active window.

19. Pressing Windows + Page Up again while a window is minimized won't return it to its former state.

20. Windows + Shift + Page Up. Press these three keys while a window is active will stretch it vertically to the maximum Desktop height. The width of the window will however stay the same. Pressing Windows + Page Down will restore it to its previous size.

21. One of the new features of Windows 7 is the ability to automatically make a window fill up half of your screen by dragging to the left or right. This pair of shortcuts performs the same function without your mouse. Once a window is fixed to one side of the screen, you can repeat the shortcut to flip it to the other side.

22. Windows + Home. This shortcut performs a similar function to hovering over a window's peek menu thumbnail in the Taskbar. The active window will stay on your Desktop while every other open application is minimized. Pressing this shortcut again will restore all the other windows.

23. Windows + E. Automatically opens up a new Explorer window to show your Libraries folder.

24. Windows + T. Like Alt + Tab, Windows + T cycles through your open programs via the Taskbar's peek menu.

25. Ctrl + Shift + Click. Hold down Ctrl and Shift while launching an application from the Taskbar or start menu to launch it with full administrative rights.

26. Ctrl + Click. Hold down Ctrl while repeatedly clicking a program icon in the Taskbar will toggle between the instances of that application, like multiple Mozilla Firefox browser windows.

27. If you are formatting an existing disk, be sure the disk does not contain any information that you need because it will be wiped off.

28. To run a program effectively, it is best to have the recommended requirements instead of just the minimum requirements. Read carefully the requirements on the outside of the software package.

29. Font management is much improved in Windows 7. Gone is the "Add Fonts" dialog , replaced with additional functionality in the Fonts folder. First, the folder shows font previews in each font file's icon (viewed with Large or Extra Large icons). Fonts from a single set will no longer show up as different fonts and are now combined as a single family.

30. If you want to silence your PC, right click the speaker icon in the notification area, then click the speaker icon.

31. You can close an open window by pressing Alt-F4 instead of using your mouse.

32. To reveal hidden memory card slots, open up My Computer. Press Alt to show the toolbar at the top of the screen, and go to Folder Options under Tools. Press the View tab and uncheck the "Hide empty drives in the Computer folder" option.

33. If some part of Windows 7 is behaving strangely, and you don't know why, then click Control Panel > Find and fix problems (or 'Troubleshooting') to access the new troubleshooting packs. These are simple wizards that will resolve common problems, check your settings, clean up your system and more.

34. If you've downloaded Windows 7 it's a good idea to create a system repair disc straight away in case you run into problems booting the OS later on. Click Start > Maintenance > Create a System Repair Disc, and let Windows 7 build a bootable emergency disc.

35. Usenet is a worldwide bulletin board system that can be accessed through the Internet or through many online services. It contains thousands of newsgroups.

36. To see what an icon does that does not have a written legend, hover your pointer over it.

37. The colors you see on your screen will vary depending on your monitor, graphics cards settings, lighting and more, yet most people use the same default Windows color profile. And that means a digital photo you think looks perfect might appear very poor to everybody else. Windows 7 now provides a Display Color Calibration Wizard that helps you properly set up your brightness, contrast and color settings, and a ClearType tuner to ensure text is crisp and sharp. Click Start, type DCCW and press Enter.

38. To rename a shortcut icon, simply right-click the icon, select Rename, and type in a new name. Press Enter.

39. When you buy software, be sure to send in the registration card. The company will then keep you posted about upgrades and future releases.

40. Perform regular housekeeping and delete those files that are no longer needed.

41. You can only cut, copy, and paste one text piece at a time. If you cut two segments in succession and then paste, you lose the first cut segment.

42. Windows 7 now combines Taskbar buttons in a way that saves space, but also makes it more difficult to tell at a glance whether an icon represents a running application or a shortcut. If you prefer a more traditional approach, then right-click the Taskbar, select Properties, and set Taskbar Buttons to "Combine when Taskbar is full". You'll now get a clear and separate button for each running application, making them much easier to identify.

43. Keep your virus protection software up to date. Most virus protection updates are available through online services.

44. By default, Windows 7 displays a plain text 'Shut down' button on the Start Menu, but it only takes a moment to change this action to something else. If you reboot your PC a few times every day then that might make more sense as a default action: right-click the Start orb, select Properties and set the 'Power boot action' to 'Restart' to make it happen.

45. If your Windows 7 Desktop has icons scattered everywhere then you could right-click it and select View > Auto arrange, just as in Vista. But a simpler solution is just to press and hold down F5, and Windows will automatically arrange its icons for you.

46. Windows 7 features interesting new ways to intelligently arrange your windows, so that (for example) if you drag a window to the top of the screen then it will maximize.

47. If you prefer the keyboard over the mouse, you will love browsing the Taskbar using this nifty shortcut. Press Windows and T, and you move the focus to the left-most icon on the Taskbar. Then use your arrow keys to change the focus to other icons, and you get a live preview of every window.

48. Click Computer in Windows 7 and you might see a strange lack of drives. Drives like memory card readers are no longer displayed if they're empty.

49. The Windows 7 magnifier offers a much easier way to zoom in on any area of the screen. Launch it and you can now define a scale factor and docking position, and once activated it can track your keyboard focus around the screen. Press Tab as you move around a dialog box, say, and it'll automatically zoom in on the currently active control.

50. If you use Windows Live Messenger a lot, you'll have noticed that the icon now resides on the Taskbar, where you can easily change status and quickly

send an IM to someone. If you prefer to keep Windows Live Messenger in the system tray, where it's been for previous releases, just close Windows Live Messenger, edit the shortcut properties and set the application to run in Windows Vista compatibility mode.

51. If your system seems unstable, or you're doing something in Explorer that regularly seems to causes crashes, then open Computer, hold down Shift, right-click on your drive and select Open in New Process. The folder will now be launched in a separate process, and so a crash is less likely to affect anything else.

52. Windows Media Player 12 is a powerful program, but it still won't play all the audio and video files you'll find online.

53. Back up frequently. If your programs have auto backup features, enable them.

54. Windows 7 has tightened up its security by refusing to run gadgets if UAC has been turned off, limiting the damage malicious unsigned gadgets can do to your system.

55. USB flash drives are convenient, portable, and very easy to lose. Which is a problem, especially if they're carrying sensitive data. Fortunately Windows 7 has the solution: encrypt your documents with an extension of Microsoft's BitLocker technology, and only someone with the password will be able to access it. Right-click your USB flash drive, select Turn on BitLocker and follow the instructions to protect your private files.

56. You can use the Aero Shake feature to minimize everything in seconds. Grab the title bar of the window you wish to keep open and give it a shake, and rejoice in a clear Desktop area.

57. The Windows 7 Media Center now comes with an option to play your favorite music, which by default creates a changing list of songs based on your ratings, how often you play them, and when they were added (it's assumed you'll prefer songs you've added in the last 30 days). If this doesn't work then you can tweak how Media Centre decides what a "favorite" tune is- click Tasks > Settings > Music > Favorite Music and configure the program to suit your needs.

58. If you seem to be typing over text instead of inserting new test, you may have depressed the Insert key. To deactivate Insert, simply press it again.

59. Hold down Shift, right-click any program shortcut, and you'll see an option to run the program as a different user.

60. When describing a CD, the term "disc" is used instead of "disk". They are pronounced the same.

61. By default Windows 7 will now automatically reduce the volume of your PC's sounds whenever it detects you're making or receiving PC-based phone calls. If this proves annoying (or maybe you'd like it to turn off other sounds altogether) then you can easily change the settings accordingly. Just right-click the speaker icon in your Taskbar, select Sounds > Communications, and tell Windows what you'd like it to do.

62. With Windows 7 we finally see system tray icons behave in a similar way to everything else on the Taskbar. So if you want to rearrange them, then go ahead, just drag and drop them into the order you like.

63. Windows 7 includes new power options that will help to improve your notebook's battery life. To see them, click Start, type Power Options and click the Power Options link, then click Change Plan Settings for your current plan and select Change Advanced Settings. Expand Multimedia Settings, for instance, and you'll see a new "playing video" setting that can be set to optimize power savings rather than performance. Browse through the other settings and ensure they're set up to suit your needs.

64. When you delete files or programs, they stay in the Recycle Bin until you empty it. Items in the Recycle Bin take up space on your hard drive.

65. If your PC seems sluggish, it's now much easier to uncover the bottleneck. Click Start, type RESMON and press Enter to launch the Resource Monitor, then click the CPU, Memory, Disk or Network tabs. Windows 7 will immediately show which processes are hogging the most system resources. The CPU view is particularly useful, and provides something like a more powerful version of Task Manager.

66. You can select a group of files by selecting the first one and then holding down the Ctrl key while you select the others.

67. A good way to practice using the mouse is to play Solitaire. You will get the feel of the mouse by clicking and dragging.

68. Some Internet Explorer add-ons can take a while to start, dragging down the browser's performance, but at least IE8 can now point a finger at the worst resource hogs. Click Tools > Manage Add-ons, check the Load Time in the right-hand column, and you'll immediately see which browser extensions are slowing you down.

69. Windows 7 will display a suitably stern warning if it thinks your antivirus, firewall or other security settings are incorrect. But unlike Vista, if you disagree, then you can turn off alerts on individual topics.

70. Macintosh and PC users can send e-mail to each other.

71. Always spell check your documents. Spell checkers will catch spelling errors, duplication errors, and most typical non-spelling errors.

72. The Windows 7 Explorer has a couple of potential annoyances. Launching Computer will no longer display system folders like Control Panel or Recycle Bin.

73. If you hold down Shift while right-clicking a file in Explorer, then you'll find the Send To file now includes all your main user folders: Contacts, Documents, Downloads, Music and more. Choose any of these and your file will be moved there immediately.

74. If you subscribe to an online mailing list, be sure you know how to un-subscribe.

75. By default Windows 7 will permanently consume a chunk of your hard drive with its hibernation file, but if you never use sleep, and always turn your PC off, then this will never actually be used.

76. If you place too many programs in Startup, it might take a minute or two before you can get to work because you have to wait for programs to load.

77. An option for displaying the time or date is to add the Clock or Calendar gadgets to the Windows Desktop.

78. If unrecoverable sectors can't be fixed using in Error Checking, they're flagged so that Windows doesn't attempt to access them anymore.

79. To turn off security messages you have to go to Control Panel -> System and Security -> Action Center -> Change Action Center Settings and you can turn off the following notifications: Windows Update, Internet Security Settings, Network Firewall, Spyware and related protection, User Account Control, Virus Protection, Windows Backup, Windows Troubleshooting, Check for updates.

80. You can easily run a program as an administrator by pressing Ctrl + Shift while opening it.

81. There is no Lock Screen button in the Start Menu anymore, so you have to press the Windows + L to lock it.

82. By default Windows 7 does show the time in 24 hour format, so if you want to get the AM / PM symbols, press the Windows Key, type "intl.cpl" to open Regional and Language Options, go to Additional Settings -> Time where Long Time is set to HH:mm and change it to HH:mm tt, for example, where tt is the AM or PM symbol (22:20 PM). To change it to the 12 hour format, you need to type it like this hh::mm tt (10:20 PM).

83. Like the Control Panel and other programs, you can also pin your favorite folders to the Taskbar for quick access. To do this, just find the folder you want, hold down on it with right-click, and drag and drop it onto the Taskbar. You will see a little prompt that says "Pin to Windows Explorer." Let go of the mouse, and you now have Windows Explorer pinned to the Taskbar. To access that favorite folder, right click on the Windows Explorer icon, and you will see the folder listed under Pinned. Just click on its name, and you are in.

84. Ctrl+Shift+N: Creates a new folder in Windows Explorer.

85. Alt+Page Up: Goes up a folder level in Windows Explorer.

86. Alt+P: Toggles the preview pane in Windows Explorer.

87. Shift+Right-click on a file: Adds Copy as Path, which copies the path of a file to the clipboard.

88. Shift+Right-click on a file: Adds extra hidden items to the Send To menu.

89. Shift+Right-click on a folder: Adds Command Prompt Here, which lets you easily open a command prompt in that folder.

90. Windows+P: Adjust presentation settings for your display.

91. Windows+(+/-): Zoom in/out.

92. Windows+G: Cycle between the Windows Gadgets on your screen.

93. Clean out your Favorites list regularly.

94. You can display a second hand on your clock by clicking the Show the Second Hand check box in the Clock settings dialog box.

95. An FM tuner is required to play live FM radio stations, while an analog or digital TV tuner is required to play and record live TV.

96. Each time you run the Upgrade Advisor, it will automatically update itself, so you get the latest changes.

97. Having the wrong time zone selected could affect the default currency symbol and the formats used for date and time displays.

98. If you cannot remember your password, you'll need someone with an administrator account to reset it for you, unless you have created a password reset disk.

99. Without Aero support, there is no Windows+Alt Flip 3D feature available.

100. When you create a new library, the file type selected depends on the type of content. General items will be selected for mixed file types.

101. For more Windows 7 information and tips, go to www.microsoft.com

PART 7

Apple Mac OS X Operating System

What Is A Mac?

A Mac is a computer made by Apple Inc. The first model in this line of computers was called The Apple MacIntosh, now just known as a Mac. It is a stand-alone computer equipped with a central processing unit (CPU), one or more disk drives, random access memory (RAM), a monitor, a keyboard and a mouse.

It comes in an assortment of colors, shapes and sizes. A Mac is a device that allows you to communicate with businesses, friends, family and strangers around the world. It helps organize all of your information such as your personal address book, your checkbook, and your photos if you have a digital camera or scanner.

Your Mac will become a teacher of new skills, games and ideas. Your Mac is YOUR personal assistant!

Is A Mac A Personal Computer (PC)?

No! Although the Mac is a computer and it is personal, the two are not the same. IBM introduced the first personal computer (PC) in 1981. Other manufacturers followed suit and they are called PCs as well. They all use a version of Microsoft Windows.

Apple took a path less traveled. Your Mac uses a different operating system than a PC. At the time of this writing, Mac OS X Snow Leopard is the most current. (OS X is pronounced Operating System Ten.)

Think of it as the difference between an audio CD and a DVD. The result is the same: beautiful music or video, playing for your enjoyment. However, CDs and DVDs are not totally interchangeable.

One advantage of having a Mac is that you can run most PC software if you install Windows. PCs on the other hand cannot run Mac software.

Different Types Of Macs

There are desktop versions and laptop versions. Desktops are not very portable but laptops were designed to be taken anywhere. Within each of those categories, there are many choices. There is a Mac to take care of you.

Every Mac uses the same operating system; some version of Mac OS. For laptops, your choices are the MacBook, MacBook Pro and the MacBook Air.

For desktops, your choices are the iMac, Mac Pro and Mac mini.

Mac OS X Operating System

The Mac OS (operating system) is the master control program for your Mac. It is the stored information that your Mac needs to operate. Without an operating system, all of the hardware would just sit there and collect dust!

Mac OS X was completely rewritten and earlier applications written for OS 9 will not work on your new machine. For an application to work on OS X, it must be written for OS X. The reason for this is older versions of the Mac OS had a classic feature which allowed many older programs to work with the new operating system. OS X does not have the classic feature.

If you are a brand new Mac user, this will not be an issue for you.

Networking

Apple makes networking the Mac easy with its Airport technologies. The Airport system allows you to set up a wired or wireless network in your home effortlessly. A network is a common group of computers connected together via a hardwired connection or a wireless connection. The purpose of the network is to be able to easily share files, printers and even access to the Internet.

A network connection can be as simple as network cable connecting two computers together. More sophisticated networks employee routers and/or wireless connections to link your computers together. Your situation and needs will dictate how much network hardware to use.

Apple Airport

Airport is Apple's networking technology that allows you to connect computers together. The Airport base station connects to the Internet source and provides wireless users access to the Internet. There is also a version that provides wired connections as well.

Macs with Airport cards installed in them can turn on their Airport cards and connect wirelessly to the Airport base station. In addition, for laptop users, the Airport card allows you to connect to Wi-Fi hotspots while you are traveling allowing you to use your laptop to connect to the Internet no matter where you are.

Getting Started

First, you need a Mac or at least access to one. Our best advice is not to spend a lot of money on your first Mac. Until you have a real good reason to have the biggest, fastest and best, stick with the entry level Mac, but one that you won't outgrow in a few months.

Mac comes in two basic versions: Laptops that are designed to be portable and desktops that are not.

Making The Connections

Keep the documentation handy. The manual that comes with the Mac will not be very big as the learning of a Mac comes from the Mac itself. There will be a guide on how to set up the Mac. It is not very difficult as there are very few wires to connect. The basics are:

- Connect the keyboard to the system box.
- Connect the mouse to the keyboard.
- If you have an Internet connection, connect the ethernet cable from the Mac to the modem.
- Plug in the power supply to the Mac and then into the wall outlet.
- If you have a printer, or any other peripheral device, you can connect it now as well.

- Now you can turn on your Mac by pressing the power button. It will look the same on almost every Mac product.

Figure 76: Power Button

Turning On Your Mac For The First Time

Press the power button. If you do not know where that is, check the written documentation. Give the Mac a few moments and you will see some activity on the screen. Assuming you are not getting a hand me down Mac from a friend or family member, you will have a few administrative details to deal with once you turn your new Mac on.

Two basic skills you will need to know for the initial setup are: moving the mouse pointer and clicking.

Mouse And Trackpad Skills

Most people will be using a mouse when interacting with their desktop style Mac. Those with laptops will be using the trackpad. Although there are differences in using the two, the commands are the same. The basic skills involved are:

- Single mouse click = one finger touch of the trackpad.
- Moving the pointer with the mouse = moving one finger along the trackpad.
- Right mouse click = two finger touch with the trackpad.
- Scrolling with a mouse ball, or using scroll arrows with the pointer = two fingers moving up/down or left/right on the trackpad.

Pointing. To point to something on the screen, move the mouse across the mouse pad until the pointer is in the spot where you want it. (For a touchpad, move your finger across the pad to do the same thing.) The pointer will move in the same direction that you move the mouse.

Clicking. One mouse click, one click, (for a touch pad, one tap) is one quick press and release of the mouse button (left mouse button if you have more than one). This is not a stabbing motion. Just smoothly press and release. Be careful that you do not move the pointer as you press the mouse. Keep your hand steady, but do not clutch the mouse as you do these tasks.

In the start-up procedure, you will need to move the pointer to Continue, and click it to move to the next screen.

- On the Welcome screen, choose your country. Click Continue.
- If you have another Mac and want to transfer files, a page will give you options to do that. As a new user, you should choose Do Not Transfer My Information Now. Click Continue.
- Next, select your keyboard layout. Click Continue.
- Enter your Apple ID or Mac member name from the iTunes or Apple Store. If you do not have an Apple ID, you can get one later. Click Continue.
- Enter all of the registration information requested. Click Continue.
- Answer the Few More Questions and decide if you want Apple to send you news, software updates and special offers. Click Continue.

You must also set up your User Account on the Create User Account screen.

- Type your name in the name box as you like to be called. ex. Jim Smith or James Smith.
- Change the Short Name entry that Mac filled in only if you want to. This is a lower case entry with no spaces or punctuation except for a dash.
- Enter a password and then type it again in the Verify box. Write it down so you do not lose it.
- Create a password reminder in the Hint box. Click Continue.
- You have now set up your account. You should now be on the Get The Full Mac Experience screen. If you have a Mac account, fill in the information, or activation key if you have bought a membership, but have not set it up yet. You do not have to buy a Mac membership at this time if you do not care to.

- Click Continue again and when your software finishes its first time start-up sequence, you will get a Thank You screen letting you know your Mac is ready to work for you.
- Click Go and you will be at your Desktop.

What Will I See After The Initial Start Up Process?

You are now at your Mac Desktop. There is a Menu Bar across the top of the screen which will always stay there, but will change appearance depending on which application is currently active. At the bottom of the screen is The Dock which holds icons for many of the applications installed on your Mac. On the right side should be an icon for your hard drive.

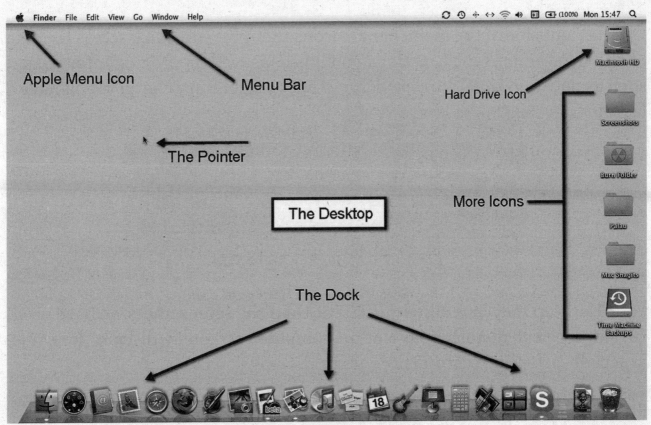

Figure 77: The Desktop

On the far left side of the Menu Bar is the Apple Menu icon. It looks like an apple with a bite out of it. This button provides system wide commands at all times independent of which application is active.

The next legend tells you what application is currently active. On the first start up, it should say Finder. Finder and the Desktop are so interwoven that they are virtually synonymous. The next few legends always pertain to the active application.

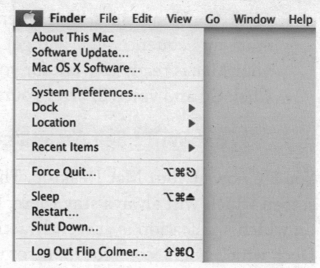

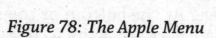

Figure 78: The Apple Menu

On the right side of the menu bar are icons that give you quick access to some of the most important functions you'll use, as well as provide information such as date and time, wireless connectivity and battery charge if you have a laptop.

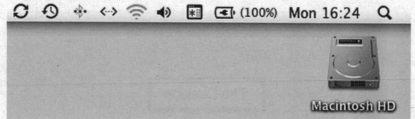

Figure 79: Menu Bar Right Side

Your Desktop may look a little different than the screen shots we have used. Do not let that disturb you. Not all computer screens will look the same, especially after you customize yours to the way you like.

Selecting Language And Country

Although you set up your country in the registration process, you may want to change your location and what language is used in the displays. Now we can use the Apple Menu for the first time and start exploring.

- Click the Apple Menu icon.
- Click System Preferences.
- In the Personal row, click Language & Text.

Here is where you can set up what language to use and what format to have for your legends in terms of date, time and currency.

Finding Your Network

Your Mac should detect if you are connected to a network. If it does not, you can help it by going to Network Preferences.

- Click on the Apple Menu icon.
- Click on System Preferences.
- In the Internet and Network (or Wireless) row, click Network.

You will have a dialog box that will help you with connecting to the Internet. For the most part though, Mac will effortlessly connect to your network, as long as you have your sign-in name and password available to the system.

Finding your network is different than setting up your e-mail account in the e-mail program. We'll get to that later.

Setting Up An Apple ID

If you have not already done so, you should set up an Apple ID. By setting up this account, you will have full access to Apple support and forums. This will help you get the most out of your Mac.

In addition, if you make use of iTunes, you will need an account there and your Apple ID will work just fine.

Controlling Access

You can password protect not only your whole computer, but if you share your computer with someone else, you can protect your files from them and they can protect their files from you.

You do this by creating different user accounts for all the folks who normally use your computer. When each account is created, that user can customize the Mac for their likes and dislikes. Their settings will not affect anyone else's, as long as everyone has their own account and log in.

Creating An Account(s)

If more than one person will be using the Mac, you can create different user accounts so that each person will have their own customized Desktop and software. To create additional user accounts:

- Click the Apple Menu icon.
- Click System Preferences.
- Click Accounts in the System line.
- If the little padlock on the bottom of the screen is locked, click it to unlock it.
- Click the Plus sign (+) to add an account.
- Fill in the information, and click Create Account.

Screen Saver

A screen saver used to be a necessity with the old CRTs. They had a habit of burning in the last image onto the screen. A screen saver was an artful way of making sure every bit of the CRT screen had some illumination. A picture, series of words or a scene was moved around the entire screen so that no one area could get the burned in effect.

We still use screen savers today, but mostly for amusement. A screen saver turns on after a predetermined amount of inactivity on your computer. You can select whatever images you care to for your screen saver. Many are included in your Mac. I use a dictionary screen saver so that every time I come back to my computer, I can learn a new word. To adjust the screen saver:

- Click the Apple Menu icon.
- Click System Preferences.
- Click Desktop & Screen Saver in the Personal line.
- Click the Screen Saver tab.

You can set up a Hot Corner to activate your screen saver. When you move the Pointer to your set up Hot Corner, the screen saver will start. To set up a Hot Corner:

- Click on the Apple Menu.
- Click on System Preferences, Desktop & Screen Saver, Screen Saver and then Hot Corners. Use the drop down menu in one of the corners for your Screen Saver start command.

Understanding The Mac Operating System

Mac OS X (the X is the Roman numeral for ten) is the name of the operating system that lets you give orders to your Mac.

Snow Leopard (OS X version 10.6) is the name of the most current release at the time of this writing. This version offers more buzzers and bells than previous versions and makes integrating your different Mac applications a breeze.

If you have used a PC, you will see many features are the same. Although there are some major philosophical differences between a Mac and a PC (Have seen those cute commercials on TV?), you will find Mac OS X easy to use.

Upgrade My Older Mac To The Newest Version

Some older Mac platforms cannot upgrade to the newest operating system. Check with Apple to see if this affects you if you are trying to upgrade.

If it does not, upgrading to the newest release of Mac OS X will give you all the newest features that Apple has created.

Desktop

The Desktop is the working area of the display and you will always have a default picture in the background. Just like your desk at home or work, this is the area where you do all your paperwork. At your desk, you pull a file, letter or checkbook from a drawer, do some work, and put it back when you are finished.

When you start your Mac the first screen you will see is the Desktop. The Finder will be the active application, unless another program is active, you will use this program to launch other applications and find and open files.

Figure 80: The Desktop

You will see the Menu Bar at the top, the Dock on the bottom, your hard drive icon on the right and if there are any open applications or files, they will be in a window on the Desktop. The active application will be listed in the Menu Bar next to the Apple Menu.

Customizing The Desktop Layout

You can change the appearance to suit your desires. You can move icons around, remove icons, add icons, change colors and so much more.

To make these changes:

- Click the Apple Menu icon.
- Click System Preferences.
- In the Personal line, the first three choices let you adjust your Desktop settings.

198

- Click on Appearance, Desktop & Screen Saver, and Dock and start making adjustments that make the Desktop look and act better for you.

Once you start accumulating icons on the Desktop, you can move them by putting the pointer on the icon, pressing down and holding the mouse button down, then dragging the icon to your desired location.

To remove an icon from the Desktop, drag it to the Trash icon in the Dock. As an option, you can right-click the icon, select Move to Trash and click that.

Figure 81: Trash Icon

Customizing Other Mac Functions

Apple gives you the ability to make many changes to most of the display settings and how different applications function. All of this is to ease the use of the Mac and to make it work the way you would like it to.

- Open the System Preferences again (that's in the Apple Menu).
- Go to each of the categories that you can look at. There is a forward and backward arrow in the upper left hand corner to help you navigate through the pages. Make some changes. See how it effects what you see.

If you are not connected to a network, or if some devices are not installed on your Mac, not all of the preference sections will apply to your machine.

Menu Bar

The Menu Bar has from left to right:

- Apple icon = System Wide Commands.
- Active Application Legend = What program is running and its associated menu.
- Menu Commands for Active Application.

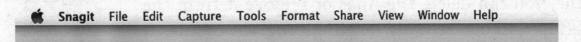

Figure 82: Menu Bar Left Side

The right side icons will be different depending on what kind of Mac you have. At a minimum, you will see:

- Speaker Icon = volume adjustments.
- Date and Time = Click and adjust here.
- Spotlight = Search for Help and Files

Figure 83: Menu Bar Right Side Volume, Date and Spotlight

Icons

An Icon is a little picture that represents a program, command or file. For instance, your hard drive icon on the Desktop actually looks like the hard drive component in your Mac. If you see a Folder Icon that means it holds other files. A File Icon is a single file that you have created.

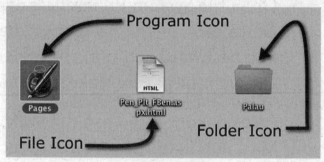

Figure 84: Icons

Icons that have a small arrow in the lower left corner are called Aliases. These are pointers to files that are stored elsewhere. This makes getting to that file easier. You can store the file anywhere, even move it. The Alias will open the file every time.

Since the Alias is simply a pointer to a specific program or file, you can delete the Alias or remove it from the Desktop without actually deleting program or file. If you want to copy the original file to a disk, don't copy the Alias. Nothing will transfer over.

Figure 85: Alias Icon

The Dock

The Dock is one of the most effective tools on your Mac. It is a row of frequently used icons displayed on the bottom of your Desktop. Apple preloads the Dock with many of the cool and groovy apps that came with your Mac. However, you can customize it to suit your needs.

The Dock has two sections, divided by dashed line near the right side of the Dock. On the left are applications and on the right are files, folders and documents that you are working on, or want to store there. There is also a Trash Can for discarding your unwanted files.

Figure 86: The Dock

Each icon represents a different program or file. Hover the pointer over each icon (that is move the pointer over the icon but do not click it) and you can see its name. Click on an icon and that program or file opens. If you open a file, its associated program opens as well.

If you see a little blue dot underneath one of the Dock's icons that means that program is already open. Just click the icon again and its window will come to the front and be active.

You can customize how the Dock looks and acts via its Preference menu. Go back to the Apple Menu, click on Dock and you can make adjustments there. You can rearrange the icons on the Dock by selecting an icon and dragging it left or right to a new position.

Adding/Removing Dock Items

To add an icon to the Dock, select the icon from the Desktop, a menu or a folder and drag it to the Dock. It will appear and stay on the Dock.

To remove an icon from the Dock, just drag it to the Desktop or the Trash.

Don't worry though. The original file or program did not get put in the Trash, just the Dock icon. You can think of a Dock icon as an Alias. If you find you do not use some of the icons on the Dock, you can move them to the Trash to make more Dock room. The only icons you cannot remove are the Finder (and why would you as the Finder is your best friend on your Mac) and the Trash.

Start Up/Shut Down

There's nothing simpler than starting a Mac. Press the power button and wait. A few screens will appear and then you will see your Desktop. When you do, you're ready to go. Sometimes you may need to restart your computer. Instead of turning it off and then starting it up from scratch, simply choose the Restart command from the Apple Menu. That will close all of the programs you are working with, shut itself down and then start itself back up.

If your Mac's screen saver has started and you want to go back to work, press any key or move the mouse and your Desktop will return.

Security Options On Start Up

Your Mac can be customized to your likings for security. To see your options:

- Click System Preferences.
- Then click Security.

If you are the only user of your Mac, then you really do not need to use many of the security features. However, if you have your Mac where it is easily accessible to strangers, you may want to use passwords to wake your Mac up or to protect your Preference settings.

You can add a password to your user account so that you are the only one who can use the computer, or protect your settings from other users.

Sleep Mode

You can put your Mac to sleep by clicking the Apple Menu, then Sleep. This is a convenient way to shut off the screen and power down the hard drive when you walk away from your Mac. If you are working on a document, you will not lose your work and you will be taken right back to where you left off if you use the sleep function.

This is not the same as turning off your Mac. When you turn off your Mac, all of the programs you were using shutdown and everything is powered down. You then have to go through the entire startup process to get your Mac back on. In the Sleep mode, your Mac will come back to life much quicker than if you went through the whole shut down process.

With a Mac laptop, closing the lid puts the Mac to sleep.

To wake up your Mac, simply press the power button. Your Mac will come alive and be right where you left off. With a laptop, open the lid and it will come alive again.

Shutting Down

You do not have to turn your Mac off every night. However, if you are finished using your Mac for a while, you can completely shut it down. Click on the Apple Menu, then Shut Down. If you do nothing at this point, at the end of one minute, your Mac will shut down. You can also select Shut Down and the Mac will immediately go through its Shut Down process.

This means that all users will be logged off before the Mac is shut down. Make sure everyone is finished using it otherwise they will just have to start it back up again.

After Start Up, What Should I See?

If you are turning your computer back on after having shut down, then you will be back at your start up Desktop. If you are waking up your Mac from a Sleep command, you will be right where you left off. Whatever files you had open, and whatever applications were open and active at the time you put the Mac to sleep will be open and active again.

Basic skills are those that are used repeatedly in every application. They include selecting text, cutting, copying, pasting and deleting text. You will also need to know how to open, close, save and print a document.

Selecting Text. Click at the beginning of the text you want to select. Hold down the mouse button and drag to the end of the text you want. Release the button and your text is highlighted. With a trackpad, click and hold with one finger and use another finger to do the drag.

Cutting and Copying Text. Once you have selected some text, you can Cut or Copy the selection and use it elsewhere. If you want to use the text elsewhere, but leave it in its original position, use the Copy Command. If you want to remove the text for use elsewhere, use the Cut command. Use either the Edit drop down menu from the Menu Bar or a right mouse click to find these two editing tools. Select the one you want. What you are doing with either command is putting this text selection on a clipboard. The clipboard stores this text for your use in the editing process.

Pasting. Once you have Cut or Copied your text, move the cursor to where you want to insert the text, and go back to the Edit menu (or right-click the mouse) and click Paste.

Deleting Text. Deleting text is different than Cutting text. If there is a selection of text you want to eliminate altogether, and you do not want to use it again, use the Delete key rather than Cut. Deleted text is not stored on the clipboard as is Cut or Copied text.

Saving a Document. One of the most important precautions you can take while working is to save your work frequently. To save your work, click on File, then Save. The first time you do this a Save dialog box will appear. If the default name is not a good name for your document, type in a name you like better. Then click Save. You can also click on the disk icon in the application's toolbar.

The Save As command allows you to make a copy of a document and rename it. This allows you to change the document yet still save an original copy. You may also be able to set up your application to automatically save your work periodically so you do not have to remember to do so. Check in the application's Preferences menu and see if you have any Save options.

Printing Your Work. From the File Menu, choose Print. After making sure all of the options are set the way you like them, click OK.

You can also use the icon on the toolbar that looks like a printer. This will start the printing process without going through the Printer Options dialog box.

Opening A File Or Application

To open a file or application, simply click its icon either on The Dock, in The Finder under Applications, its shortcut icon on the Desktop or wherever you have stored it.

Any time you start an application, or choose a document to view, it will open in a new window. If you have selected a document, not only will the document appear, but it will also have started the application it was created with. If you start an application, the application will start but no document will be selected. You can either start a new document, or by clicking File then Open, select from recently used documents created by this application.

Re-sizing A Window

When you first open a window, it will most likely not fill the whole screen. If you like it that way, there is no reason to change it. However, sometimes the smaller sized windows are not as easy to view and you might not see everything that is in the window. If you have scroll bars in a window that is telling you that there is more to see.

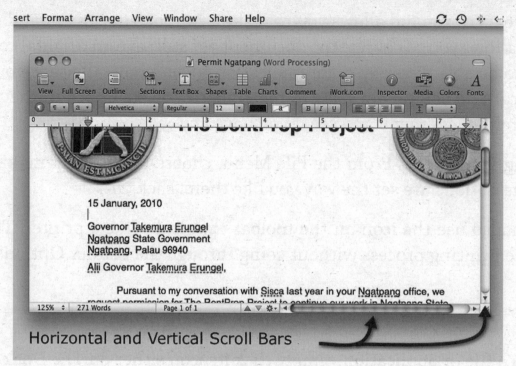

Figure 87: Scroll Bars

One way to make the window larger is to click the green dot in the upper left corner of the window. You will see a plus sign when the pointer gets to it. Click the green dot and the window will go to its default full setting. If this is not big enough, you can manually make your window larger.

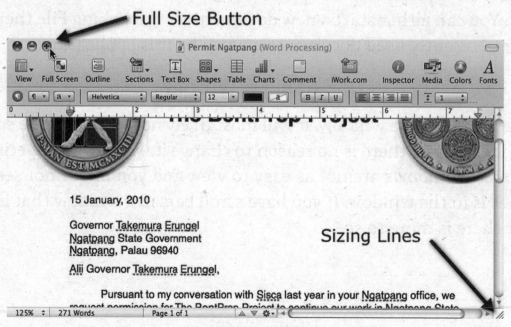

Figure 88: Sizing

To make your window larger, point to the lines in the lower right corner of the window, press and hold the mouse button down and drag the window to the size you want. If the window is too big, you can use this method to make it smaller. Your Mac will remember how you like your window and open that way the next time you open it.

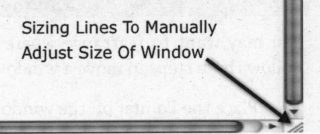

Sizing Lines To Manually Adjust Size Of Window

Figure 89: Sizing Lines

You can also make a window disappear from the screen, but still have it instantly available to you. You can minimize the window by clicking the yellow dot in the upper left corner of the window. When you move the pointer to the yellow dot, a minus sign will appear. Click it and the window will move onto the Dock in the right hand section. Clicking its icon on the Dock will return it to the Desktop.

Figure 90: Close (X), Minimize (-) and Maximize (+) Buttons

The red close (X) dot in your window will close the file you are working on, but not necessarily the application you are working with.

Open any document. Notice the application is listed in the Menu Bar. Now just close the document with the red dot or the File Menu Exit Command. Notice that the application is still listed in the Menu Bar.

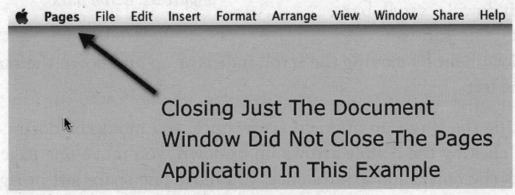

Closing Just The Document Window Did Not Close The Pages Application In This Example

Figure 91: Closing Document Only

Moving A Window

You may want to rearrange where a window is located on your Desktop. Follow these steps to move a window:

- Place the Pointer on the window's title bar.
- Drag the title bar to the location you and release the mouse button.

Notice that when you move a window, the Menu Bar at the top stays put while the Tool Bar for the document you are working on moves with the window. The Menu Bar will always show you which application is the active application. It may still be the active application even though you have closed all of the documents you were working with in that application.

Scroll Bars

A Scroll Bar is a blue button in a vertical slide or horizontal slide with arrows to control the direction of movement. It is on the right side of the screen for vertical scrolling and on the bottom for horizontal scrolling.

When a document or Web page is so big that it cannot be completely displayed in a window, a scroll bar appears. You can see the

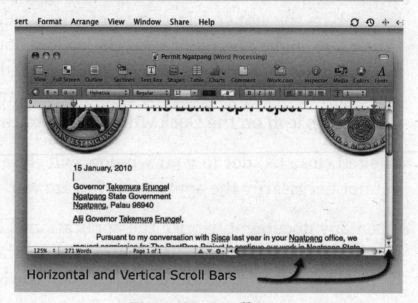

Horizontal and Vertical Scroll Bars

Figure 92: Scroll Bars

entire document by moving the scroll indicator up and down the screen, or right and left.

By clicking the single up or down arrow once, you move the document one line. By clicking the double arrows up or down, you move one page. When you click the horizontal arrows once, you move one space left or right. You can also drag the indicator in either scroll pane and rapidly move through a document.

The Mac gives you a choice of how to show the scroll arrows. You can cluster them at the bottom right corner of screen, or split off the up arrow to the top of the vertical scroll bar and the left scroll arrow to the left side of the scroll bar. Completely your choice. You make this choice in the Appearance tab of the System Preferences in the Apple Menu.

Tab Buttons

The tab key of your Mac keyboard works just like it did with a typewriter: it moves the cursor a number of spaces from left to right. It can also move from box to box when you are in a document with fields, or a Web page with fields.

However, Tab Buttons allow you to select from different sections of a dialog box. For example, when you select System Preferences from the Apple Menu, you will have a number of Tab Buttons representing different windows you can open to make adjustments. If any application has a Preferences selection from its menu, you will see more Buttons.

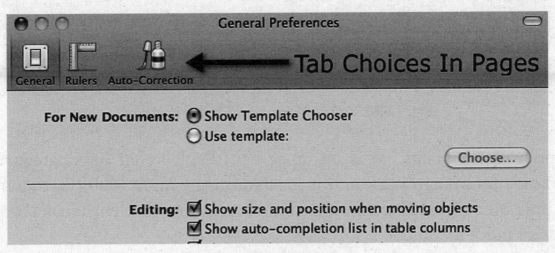

Figure 93: Tab Buttons

Menus

A menu is a list of commands or options displayed on your screen, which allows you to perform a myriad of tasks.

Just as you would select your choices from a restaurant menu, you select your choices of what to do on your computer.

The most frequently used menus are the Apple Menu and the Finder Menu. You will access all of your system wide commands, and create and maintain your file structure with these two menus.

Figure 94: Apple Menu and Finder Window

An application's menu bar is an on-screen display that lists categories of commands for an application. It is located on the main Menu Bar alongside the Apple Menu icon. You may have a toolbar below that with icons for commands or more menus.

Menu Bar

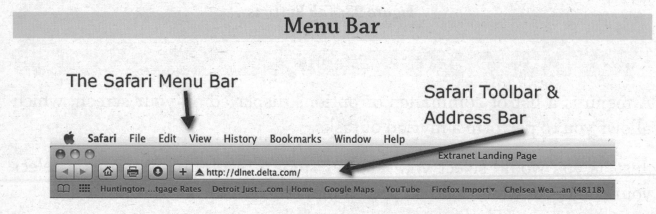

Figure 95: Safari Menu and Toolbar

The Menu Bar gives you access to the active application's commands. You will use these to create, edit, manage and manipulate documents and files. When you are in a word processing application, the menu commands will be different then when you are working in your Web browser. However, menus and sub-menus work the same way from application to application.

Menus And Sub-menus

Each application has its own menu for doing all sorts of tasks.

When you click on any menu, a small box drops down giving you optional commands to work with. Once you have selected an option by clicking on it, if it has an arrow on the right side, you will be given more options in another menu. This is called opening a sub-menu. All of these are windows that open and close as you use them. You are just being given more options on how to do your task at hand.

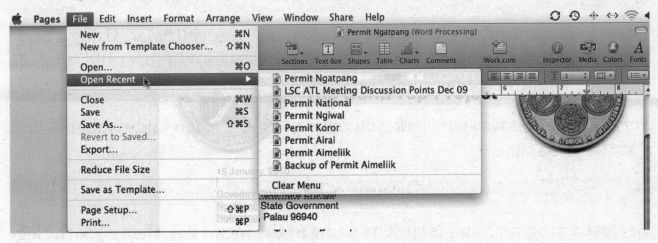

Figure 96: Menu and Sub-menu

Shortcut Menu (Secondary Menu)

Many, if not all objects on the screen will have a secondary menu of actions you can accomplish through the mouse. To activate this menu, simply right-click the mouse. The menu, if one exists will pop up. Then click the feature you want to use.

Remember, if you have a trackpad, a right-click is done by using two fingers on the trackpad.

Function Keys

The Function Keys are the top row of keys on your keyboard that have the labels F1 through F12. In addition, in that row of keys, are the Escape Key (esc) and the Eject Key.

The F1 through F12 Function Keys are programmable keys. They provide special functions depending on the software you are using. For example, F12 brings up the Dashboard. While writing in my word processing program, F2 brings up a spreadsheet formula tool bar. Check your applications Help Menu to see what the Function Keys do.

Control, Option And Command Keys

These keys are located outboard of the spacebar. Conveniently, they are labeled control, option and command. There is only one control key but the option and command keys are located on both sides of the spacebar.

These keys are used to give you more command over your Mac. Using a combination of these keys with the other keyboard letters, numbers and symbols gives you a much broader number of commands.

For example, to save your work, you could press the command symbol ⌘ and S at the same time.

Closing A Program

To close a program, simple click its name in the Menu Bar, then click the legend that says Quit with the program name.

This is different than closing a document. To close a document, but leave the program running, click File, then click Save (to make sure you save your work) and then either click File again and then Close, or simply click the red close button in the upper left corner of the window.

Frozen Computer

At some point, your Mac will freeze up. It does not happen often, and you certainly did not do anything to make this happen. It just is in its nature to sometimes stop working.

First off, give it a few minutes to sort itself out. If that does not work, try closing the file and program. If that does not work, you can use the Force Quit command from the Apple Menu.

Open the Apple Menu and click Force Quit. A list of applications will pop up. Pick the one that is causing you the problem. Mac will force the program to close. You will lose any data that was not saved prior to the freeze.

Mac Tasks

Dialog Box

A dialog box is an on-screen message box or window that enables you to choose options and send other information to a program. It conveys information to, or requests information from the user.

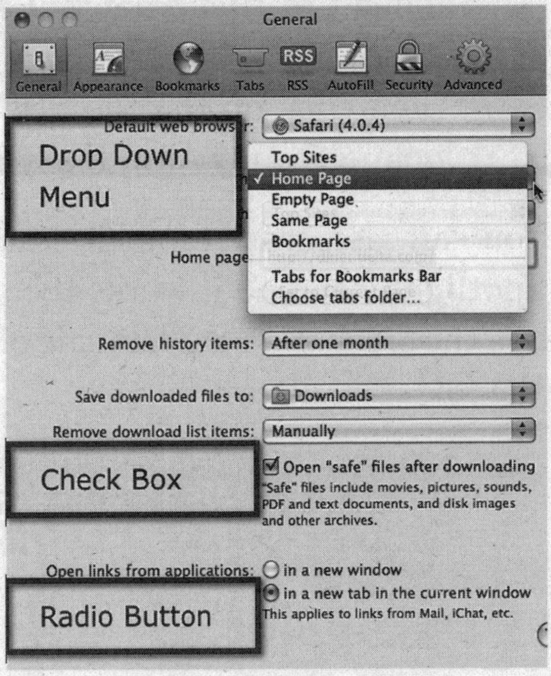

The Mac does its best to do what you want it to do. When it is asked to do something and it needs more information, it starts a dialog with you to see what your intentions are, or to give you a choice on how to do something. The dialog gives you control over how the Mac does your tasks.

Figure 97: Dialog Box

Sometimes the dialog box gives you a drop down menu to make choices from, sometimes you have to click a radio button to make the choice and sometimes you have boxes to choose from.

To find a file or folder:

Figure 98: Spotlight File Search

- You can use the Spotlight search function. In the upper right hand corner of the Menu Bar is a little magnifying glass.
- Click that icon and the Spotlight Search Box opens.
- Start typing what you are looking for. For example, start typing Aunt Mary. All of the contents on your Mac that have what you are typing in the title will start to be displayed. Keep typing until the list is small enough to find what you are looking for.
- Then click on the file title and it will open. In our example, we were looking for my Aunt Mary 3 letter.

You can also search for Files and Folder through the Finder. It also has a Spotlight icon and it works the same way as on the Menu Bar. You can also use the Sidebar on the left side of the Finder window to manually go through the folder structure.

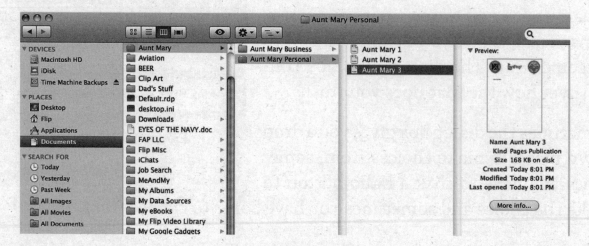

Figure 99: Finder File Search

For example, if you are looking for that letter to Aunt Mary, click on the Finder, then Click on Documents in the Sidebar. Each time you click on the Sidebar, the results show in the main window called the Detail Pane. You should then find your Aunt Mary folder. Open that and your Aunt Mary letter should be there.

Finder

The Finder is Mac's way of being able to look throughout your entire Mac and find Files, Folders and Applications. The Finder is a powerful tool you should become very familiar with.

To activate the Finder: either click on its icon on the Dock, or anywhere on the Desktop where there is not another window. You will see the Finder legend in the Menu Bar.

Figure 100: Finder Icon

If a Finder window does not open on the Desktop with Finder in the Menu Bar, click Command (the ⌘ on your keyboard) N and a new Finder window opens.

The title of the folder that is open in the Finder window is listed in the top center on the Title Bar.

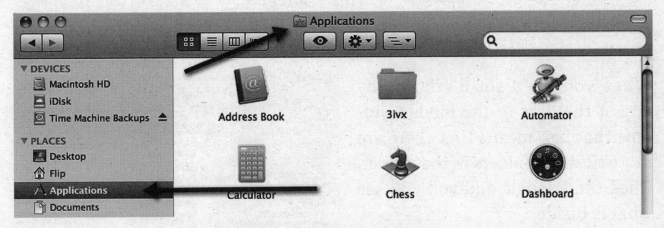

Figure 101: Finder Title Bar

Below that are a row of tools that allow you to control how the Finder shows you the folder structure and how to navigate through that structure. The left and right arrows allow you to go forward and backward through the Finder as you select different folders. The four buttons grouped together are the view buttons.

The Finder gives you four different views where folders and files reside on your Mac. You can choose to have a lot of information shown including when a folder was created, how big it is or even what program created it. Or you can just see an icon of the folder. It is your choice. One even makes your Mac mimic your iPod and gives you a cover flow look to the files.

The next button, the Quick Look Eye, allows you to look at information about the folder that is selected. The Action button that looks like a gear, has commands that are frequently used to manage your files and folders. The last button that looks like an indented list will show you the location of what you are looking at within the entire filing structure of your Mac. The Spotlight search bar works in the Finder just as it does everywhere else.

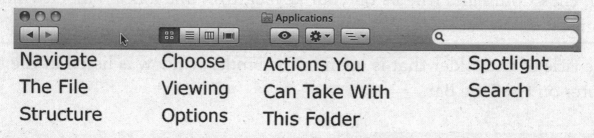

Figure 102: Finder Buttons

When you see a small triangle by any of the lists in the Finder window that just means that there are more files and folders in that folder. Click the triangle and you will see what is inside.

Figure 103: Small Triangle Means More Files In The Folder

Renaming A File Or Folder

You should get in the habit of naming files and folders with meaningful names right from the start of your Mac experience. However, you will find occasion where you will have to rename a file or folder. If you do, the short way is to click on the file name, pause then click it again. It should change to blue the second time and you can type in the new name. Then click the Return key and the new name will be applied.

Copying And Moving A File Or Folder

Copying and moving files and folders is a snap with your Mac. Let's discuss copying first. The easiest way is to use the mouse.

• Select a file or folder that you want to copy.
• Right-click the mouse and from this menu.
• Select Copy "the actual name of your file".
• Then go to the location you want to place this copy, right- click again.
• Click Paste. A copy of your file will appear. Be careful about trying to copy an Alias, thinking it is your file. Make sure you have the correct icon.

To move a file or folder, you simply select it, press and hold down the mouse button and drag the file or folder to its new location.

Creating A Folder

To create a new folder:

• Right-click on an empty area of the Desktop, or in an empty area of the directory you want to store this new folder in. A menu will appear.
• Click on New Folder. Then give your folder a title and you're done.

You can also do this from the File Menu in almost any Window. Click File, then New Folder. In some menus, only New will show. Click that and you will be given a list of possibilities, one of which is Folder.

Deleting Files And Folders

Deleting files and folders is also a snap. Simply find its icon either on the Desktop or in a directory. Make sure it is selected. Then right-click on it and select Move To Trash, or use the File Menu in the Menu bar and select Move To Trash.

You can also drag the icon to the Trash bin located on the Dock.

Playing A CD Or DVD

Your Mac is designed to make entertainment easy. Simply insert your CD into the CD/DVD drive and iTunes will automatically open.

It will first ask if you want to import the tracks to your Mac for storage. This is a very handy way to get your music library onto your Mac for future use. If you do, select Import and iTunes will do the rest. If your songs do not start playing automatically, press the play button after the first song has been imported. We'll chat more about iTunes later.

To play a DVD, simply insert it into the CD/DVD drive. The first time you do this, you will need to set the region of the world you are in. A dialog box will open. Select your region and then your DVD will start playing. A small control panel will open giving you controls similar to the controls of any DVD player.

Apple QuickTime

Apple QuickTime Player, included with Mac OS X, is an audio and video file playback system. If you have an audio or video file, rather than a disk, QuickTime is what will play the file for you. It is a powerful multimedia playback application and you will get to know it well if you receive audio or video files from friends or websites.

Applications And Programs

Programs are those hunks of computer software that make everything run in your Mac. For example, Mac OS X is a program.

An application is a bit of software written for a particular purpose or for a particular "application". Quicken is a checkbook application. It has many more features than that, but I think you get the idea between a specific purpose application and a system program. For our general use purposes, you can use the terms interchangeably.

Mac Programs

Mac programs are those bits of software written in the Mac programming language. Mac programs will not run on a PC computer. Your Mac comes with a suite of programs called iLife. This has the programs you will use most often such as Mail, iTunes, iPhoto and so much more.

Can I Run A PC Program On My Mac?

PC programs are written in the Windows programming language. Mac computers are capable of using PC applications as long as you use some special software that comes with your Mac called BootCamp, or purchase a different program called Parallels. You must also have a copy of Windows XP, Vista or Windows 7 installed on your Mac.

BootCamp allows you to start your Mac in PC mode. Parallels allows you to run a PC environment concurrently with your Mac environment.

If you are new to computers you will not need to use this function. If you have switched from a PC and just cannot give up some of your software, you can get more detailed instructions from Apple on the use of either Boot Camp or Parallels. One inconvenient note though. You must have a fresh copy of Windows to install on your Mac. The disc that came with your PC with the Windows operating system on it, just in case you needed to reinstall it, cannot be used.

Adding An Application

Adding an application to your Mac is easy. Simply insert the software disk into your CD/DVD drive and the installation process should start automatically. You will have some dialog boxes pop up giving you choices during the installation process. For the most part, just use the default settings that are already in the boxes. Answer all the questions that may pop up during installation and then when the last screen goes away, you'll be ready to use your new program.

If you've downloaded a program, you start the installation process by double clicking its icon in the Downloads folder.

Deleting An Application

Simply send its icon to the Trash as you would any file or folder. Many applications take up lots of storage space. Until you Empty The Trash, it is just being stored in a different place on your Mac. Remember to empty the trash frequently.

Starting An Application

With your Mac, an application can be started in one of two ways. If you click the application's icon, it will start.

You can also open a file of any sort and the application it was created with will also open. No need to remember how you created any particular file. The file knows and will always open with the correct application.

Quitting An Application

You quit an application by clicking on its name in the Menu Bar, then clicking Quit. That will close the application and any files you are working on with it.

This is different than quitting a file. For example, if I am writing a letter to Aunt Mary and quit the application I am using, both the application and the letter close. If I just quit the letter to Aunt Mary through the File drop down menu, then Exit, only the letter to Aunt Mary closes. The application stays open.

Word Processing Overview

Your Mac comes with a basic word processing program called TextEdit. It allows you to create documents in either a plain text format or Rich Text Format. Rich text allows you to use added features such as bold lettering, italics or styles.

Once you have created a document, you can go back into it and edit it by highlighting what you want to change or remove, using the skills we introduced previously: pointing, selecting, dragging and use of edit commands. Apple makes a fully functional word processing program called Pages. It comes in the iWork suite of software.

Spreadsheet Overview

Although the Mac does not come with a spreadsheet in its basic software, iWork is Apple's suite of programs that includes a very powerful spreadsheet program conveniently named, Numbers. Numbers allows you to select a template for your spreadsheet, helps you create formulas for its calculations and interacts with the other programs in iWork so that you can display your work in other documents.

Games

Your Mac comes with a Chess game pre-installed. However, there are a gazillion games out there for your Mac. And there is no reason not to have fun with your new machine. Check out www.apple.com/games.

Dashboard

The Dashboard is a powerful tool in the Mac world. The Dashboard holds Widgets. Widgets are small programs designed to do small, but powerful tasks such as get you the weather, play a game or check your stocks. There are a number of Widgets pre-installed on your Mac and more are available to use.

There are two ways to see the Dashboard. You can click on its icon in the Dock, or press the F12 key (key may vary depending on your keyboard). The Dashboard pops up and you will notice that what you were working on gets a gray tone to it and you cannot work on it. To hide the Dashboard: click your mouse in the gray background, or press the F12 key again.

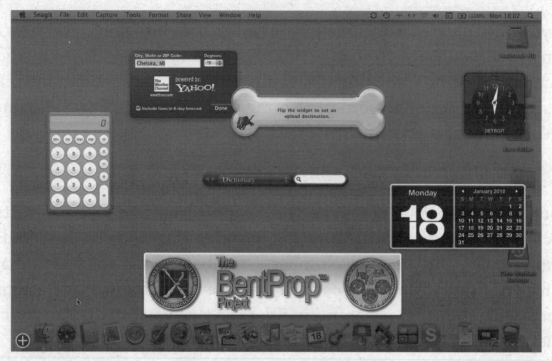

Figure 104: The Dashboard

To add or subtract widgets:

- Open the Dashboard.
- Click the little Plus Sign on the lower left of the Desktop. It rotates and is now seen as an X. A row of widgets will appear and you can pick and choose the ones you want. When you are finished, click the X and it turns back into the Plus Sign.
- To remove a widget: Click the Plus Sign in the lower left corner. Each Widget now has a little X in the upper left corner of the Widget. Click that X and the Widget disappears.
- When you are done, click the X in the lower left portion of the Desktop and your widgets will be ready for you.

Mail

Your Mac includes a first class e-mail program called Mail. It is simple to use and the editing tools are powerful enough for most e-mail needs. It works seamlessly with other Mac programs so importing photos and attaching documents is a snap.

To use mail, you will need a way to connect to the Internet and an ISP. If you've already set up your network, you're almost done.

To open Mail, simply click its icon on the Dock. You can also click its icon in the applications list. The first time you open Mail, it will help you setup your first e-mail account. You will need to know your e-mail account settings in order to fill in the set up screens. You will need to know your account login name, e-mail address, POP and SMTP settings and your password. Once mail has these settings, you should be good to go.

What Is Safari?

Safari is Apple's Web browser (also available for the PC). Safari is a full featured Web browser that allows you to get the full impact of the multimedia World Wide Web: audio, video, news feeds and so much more.

Using Safari will allow you to connect to libraries around the world, check on the latest news, watch movies and television shows on your computer and so much more.

Once you have an Internet Connection and an ISP, to start your surfing experience, just click the Safari icon on the Dock.

How Do I Keep Track Of Websites I Want To Revisit?

You can keep track of your favorite websites via the Bookmark function in Safari. Other browsers may use the term Favorites instead of Bookmarks.

When you find a site that you want to save for easy access, click the + sign on the Safari Toolbar. A dialog box will open asking you to type a name for the website (its address will be there by default, but you may want a shorter name for convenience) and select a location to store the Bookmark. If you plan on using this Bookmark frequently, you can even put it on the Bookmark Menu bar that is displayed under the Safari buttons.

Are Macs At Risk For Viruses, Spyware, Malware And Adware?

The good news is that Macs for the most part are immune from viruses written for PCs. However, since Macs can run PC software, a Mac can still be a carrier of viruses unless you practice safe computing at all times.

Since Mac operating systems are just a small percentage of the operating systems that are out there, most of the bad folks write their viruses in the PC language. Very few viruses have been found in the Mac language. If you plan on using any PC programs on your Mac, you should get a good, full featured anti-virus program to help protect your Mac. There are Mac anti-virus programs coming on line as the future needs for this may grow.

Ending An Internet Session

To end an Internet session, log off the website if it required a password to get in and simply close your browser. Remember, you should close out the browser completely with the Safari Menu, File Menu Quit command. Just closing the current window with the red button might keep other browser windows open in the background if you happen to have had a few open.

If you have a dial-up Internet connection, and if you have not set up Safari to automatically dial-up when you open your browser, you will need to manually turn off the modem.

iChat

Instant Messaging (IM) is a real time, typed conversation between computer users using the Internet. Apple's iChat is Mac's IM software. However, to say iChat is just for instant messaging is to downplay what you can do with it.

Apple's iChat also allows you to do live video messaging. Depending on your model, your Mac may have a built in video camera that allows you to add "you" to the chat medium. Of course the other user needs to have a video camera as well for this to all work out, but you are on your way to having video phone calls without having to pay any extra telephone charges to anywhere in the world.

You access iChat via the Dock or the applications list.

Address Book

The Address Book is a highly integrated component in your Mac. You keep track of all of your contacts in an easy to use format and every program that needs access to that information goes to the same place. Gone are the days of multiple address lists for different programs.

You can also easily create mailing lists, or groups, by creating a group name and adding individual names to that list. This is a very handy way to send out the same message to a related group of people.

To start your address list:

- Open the Address Book either from the Dock or the applications menu. You will notice three columns: Groups, Names and Card Entries.
- Click the little plus sign below the Names column and the fields in the right column will become active.
- Fill in the fields and click Edit. The name now appears in the Names list.
- To edit an already existing entry, highlight the name in the names list.
- Click Edit in the entry column. When you are finished editing, click Edit again.

To create a Group:

- Click the plus sign in that column.
- Name the Group.
- Drag names from the Names Column to the Group. The name will now appear in both places.

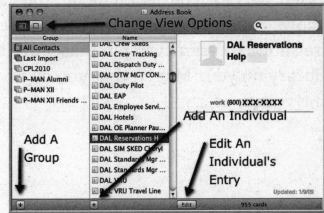

Figure 105: Address Book

iCal

The calendar program in your Mac is called iCal. It is a powerful time management tool. It allows you to color code appointments so that you can keep better track of what you are doing and why. With daily, weekly and monthly views, you'll be able to see what you are doing and when. You can give yourself alarms to remind you to get going and not be late. The easy to use buttons and tabs make creating your calendar easy and therefore more likely that you will actually follow it. To start iCal, click its icon in the Dock.

Preview

Preview is a tool that allows you to open documents, photos and other files as well as take screenshots of what is on your Mac's screen. This is especially handy when you receive a file attached to an e-mail and want to look at it without saving it to your computer.

Preview will open a PDF or document, and will open an image file with iPhoto. Preview will automatically start if you click the Quick View Icon in the attachment line of an e-mail.

iTunes

The iTunes program is a wonderful tool for managing your music and video files for playback on your Mac, iPod or iPhone. In addition, it will connect to the iTunes store via the Internet allowing you to purchase audio and video files for your enjoyment. You can download your favorite television shows from yesteryear, or the episode you missed last week of your favorite show. You can even purchase full length movies. You can store your CD library on your Mac so that you do not have to hassle with discs for choosing your music.

iPhoto

The iPhoto program does for digital photography what iTunes does for music and video. With iPhoto, you can import images from a camera, scanner or file, edit them, organize them in albums and export them by e-mail, printed photo or a file. With iPhoto, you have an integrated system that works seamlessly with your Mail and TextEdit programs so you can create great letters with photos.

When you connect a digital camera to your Mac, the process will begin automatically to help you download the photos into the Mac and help you organize the images for easy access in the future.

Open iPhoto, then click on the Tutorial Link in the Help menu and get in depth lessons on how to use iPhoto.

iMovie

The iMovie application is a great way to import, edit and store camcorder files that you have taken or have been given to you. You can be your own movie editor and create works of moving art. Open iMovie, then click on the Tutorial Link in the Help menu for in depth lessons on how to use iMovie.

Spaces

Spaces is a way to extend your Desktop without cluttering it. Another way to look at it is that you can create customized desktops with certain applications open in them, without having to have them all open in one Desktop screen.

For example, you can create a Space that has Safari and Mail and FireFox open in it. You can create another Space with iPhoto and Pages open. By simply switching from Space to Space, you can work in the programs you like without having to open them all in one screen.

The first time you open Spaces you will have to make some selections. To start Spaces, click its icon on the Dock. Click the Set Up Spaces button. You will now be on the Expose & Spaces Preferences window. Click the Spaces tab and check the box Enable Spaces.

You can pick how many rows and columns you want which sets up how many Spaces you have.

Once you have done that, when you click on Spaces in the Dock, your current Desktop will disappear and your Spaces will appear. Click the Space that has the selection of programs you want. I find that by organizing some of my programs into one space, I can work faster and easier. I can quickly get my e-mail and use both Web browsers for the work I need to do each day. When I write, I like to put photos into my work. That's why I have a Space with Pages, my word processing program, and iPhoto together. When I see my collection of Spaces, I click on the one I want and my Desktop comes back with those applications open.

Initially your Space will be blank. Just open the programs you want and that will assign them to that Space.

Time Machine

Time Machine is Mac OS X's backup system. It backs up all of your files the first time you elect to do that, and then just backs up the changes to your files each time you back up.

If you lose a file, you just go back through the Time Machine until you find the file you are looking for.

It is best to back up to an external hard drive. If you create a Time Machine back up on your Mac's hard drive, and if your Mac's hard drive dies, you will have lost all of your data.

File Management

File Management Styles

From the start, you should keep track of your files and folders in an intelligent manner. Some folks like to have every file visible. Others like to put similar files into folders and then open the folder to see all of the files in it. Some folks want an Alias on the Desktop for each file and others want a clean Desktop and use the directories to find files.

It really does not matter so long as you know how to find your files. Your Mac makes it easy by showing you recently used items in the Dock as well as allowing you to file items how you want to.

The hot ticket though is to always name your files with meaningful names no matter how you are going to store them.

Name Structure Hints

Every time you create a file, use a name that relates to the file, and one that you will be able to recall. No matter what program you are working with, the program you use to create the file will always be attached to it. You will not have to remember what program belongs to which file. In the Windows world, when you saved a file, the extension was automatically added to the name you applied to the document. For example, ThisDocument.doc. If you save a Windows created document to your Mac, you will see the extensions such as .doc, .pdf, .kmz etc. But for your Mac documents, you will not see these extensions.

To check on this sort of information when you are working in a document, you can click on File, then Properties. If you are in a directory of your files, you can right-click on its icon and then click Get Info.

Backing Up

The best way to back up your Mac files is automatically with Time Machine. You will see why it's called Time Machine at the end of this section. It is best to use an external hard drive for your backups. If you backup to your Mac's internal hard drive, you risk losing everything if your Mac has a problem.

When you connect an external hard drive to your Mac, a Time Machine dialog box should open up. Once the setup is complete, it will take a few hours for the first backup to complete. If possible, let the first backup run completely uninterrupted. All subsequent backups will take less time as they will only backup differences.

If you lose all your files on your hard drive, you can get everything back from your backup drive. Even better though, if you discard a file, you can retrieve it since you can go back in time and get it from the Time Machine backup.

101 Mac Tips And Tricks

1. If you want to delete forward on a Mac, hold the Function key (FN) while pressing Delete.

2. The Command key has a flower-like symbol on it. It functions like the Control key on a Windows keyboard.

3. If you miss Control+Alt+Delete, you can end slow applications on the Mac by pressing Command+Option+Escape to force programs to quit.

4. On Mac laptops right-click by using two fingers on the trackpad (it's easiest with your pointer and middle fingers) and click the trackpad.

5. With Snow Leopard's Quick Look, you no longer have to drag items from the trash in order to view them. While in the trash folder, hit Command+Y while on any file to see a preview of its contents.

6. Want to change an icon to something more to your liking? First, find the icon you want. Then click on it, and hit Command+C to copy it. Click on the icon you want to change, and use Command+I to launch the folder info. Click on the old icon in the folder and use Command+V to paste the new icon.

7. If you want to open an address in a new tab without deselecting your current tab, type the address into the address bar, then press Command+Enter. This allows you to work easily in multiple tabs.

8. If you want to see what a font looks like, you don't have to open Font Book or a font manager. In Cover Flow, a font icon will appear as a small, two-letter sample of the font you have selected. To see a larger sample of the font, select a font file and use Quick Look (Command+Y) to see it, or just hit the spacebar.

9. You can choose to view your stack in either a fan or a grid view. To change it, click on a stack until a menu appears. Then, select "View As" and choose either Fan or Grid. The stack will then open with your preferred style.

10. Reading PDFs becomes infinitely easier in Preview if you select "Continuous Scrolling": then you don't move from page to page, but read an infinitely long "scroll" which allows you to zoom in as much as you desire (good for older eyes).

11. Pressing Esc while typing in most applications pops up a list of suggested completions of the word you're typing.

12. Image Capture lets you manage photos on your camera before you download them.

13. Right-click on an open PDF in Safari to get the context menu which includes the option to open the PDF in Preview.

14. Pressing the Tab key in Exposé cycles through open applications.

15. Dragging a Window to the extreme edge of the screen and holding it there will trigger you to move to the next "Space". After pressing F8, pressing "C" will collect all windows into Space 1. Pressing C again reverses it.

16. Press Command-Q to close applications when command-tabbing. This is possibly the fastest way you'll find to close several applications in quick succession.

17. Macs with remote controls can be put to sleep by holding down the play button on the remote.

18. Triple-click selects a whole paragraph of text.

19. To select a block of text, click the start position, then Shift-click the end position. Significantly, this doesn't just work in editing applications like Word (where you might be already doing it anyway), but it also works with non-editable text, such as a web page in Safari.

20. In TextEdit, Option-click & drag selects a rectangle of text.

21. When entering text in applications such as Text Edit, Mail, and iChat, you can turn to the built in auto-correct and text substitution tools for a better and faster experience. Text substitutions macros that you can enter and the software will self type a longer phrase (you can define the macros and phrases from the "Language and Text Preferences" window). Control + click in the text entry field for turning these features on or off.

22. Command click the jelly bean found in the top right corner of some applications to cycle through toolbars.

23. In Safari, Command-Shift-click a link opens it in a new tab and immediately displays the page.

24. Hold the Option key while clicking the Zoom button (green button, rightmost of three in the top left corner of windows) switches the zoom state of all windows in the selected application.

25. Option-click the minimize button minimizes all windows in the application.

26. Option-click on a minimized window will restore all windows for that application.

27. Option-click on a running application in the Dock hides the front-most application and brings the clicked application to the front (unless it already was).

28. Option-click on the close tab icon in Safari, closes all other tabs. Handle this one with care – there's no warning dialog.

29. Option-arrow moves cursor by word.

30. When menus are selected, press the option key to reveal alternative functions.

31. When you use separate user accounts, Mac OS X's securities features help you to keep each user's files secure from all other users.

32. When you position the Dock vertically on the left or right of the screen, application shortcuts appear above the divider bar, folder and document shortcuts appear below the divider bar, and the Trash appears at the bottom.

33. If your user name doesn't appear at the right end of the menu bar, your Mac isn't configured for Fast User Switching, and you can't switch users.

34. When you open the Desktop & Screen Saver pane of System Preferences, Mac OS X displays the tab you used last.

35. From the Sound Effects tab of the Sound pane in System Preferences, you can also control whether Mac displays the Volume icon at the right end of the menu bar.

36. Applying a background color or picture to a Finder window can help you pick that window out more easily from other Finder windows.

37. Searching filenames is much faster than searching contents, so if you can remember enough of the name of the file you want, try searching by filename first.

38. You can launch Quick Look for the selected file or files by pressing the Spacebar.

39. When buying writable or recordable media, put quality above price. Your data is valuable!

40. PPP is the abbreviation for Point-to-Point Protocol, the network protocol used for connecting to the Internet via dial-up.

41. If you see an address in an e-mail message that you want to add to your address book, Control-click or right-click the address and click Add to Address Book.

42. To see which updates you've installed on your Mac, click the Installed Updates tab of the Software Update pane.

43. For a laptop Mac, you can select the Show Battery Status in The Menu Bar check box to display a battery readout in the menu bar.

44. If the underside of your Mac laptop gets too hot, try using the Reduced Processor Performance setting to decrease the amount of heat output.

45. If you're short of disk space you might prefer to keep a compressed file containing downloading software instead of the disk image file. But you'll save the most space by deleting both the disk image and the compressed file.

46. When playing a playlist, you can randomize the order of the songs by clicking the Shuffle button once.

47. In the menu bar you can check the status of your battery, and hopefully you won't see "Service Battery."

48. If you're running Tiger on your machine, don't worry. You can install Snow Leopard without having Leopard installed on your Mac first.

49. Showing the date in the menu bar can prove to be useful sometimes and it can be done as simple as entering the "Date and Time Preferences" menu and adjusting the settings.

50. Apple Stores provide in-store training on all of their products. The Apple Store Website has lots of tutorials to help you make the most use of your Mac.

51. Automatically set your Mac's time zone. Navigate to the Date And Time preference in System Preferences and check off "Set time zone automatically using current location."

52. If you have something planned on your Google or/and Yahoo calendars, it can be a good idea to import them into Snow Leopard. Add a new account under the iCal preferences, select the server and you are done.

53. Synchronizing the contacts with your iPhone and Mobile Me is a snap. Now you can sync your Gmail and Yahoo! address books so you can talk to your contacts and get the contact info. Go to the Contact preferences, click the Accounts tab and then click the Accounts tab. Press the configure button and follow the instructions provided.

54. Just about any USB keyboard works on the Mac even if the keyboard was originally designed to work on a PC.

55. You no longer have to buy the QuickTime Pro application to be able to edit and convert videos. This can now be done without any fee in QuickTime X.

56. If your computer is password protected, when it goes to sleep for a certain time, Snow Leopard will ask for the password. Enter the Security Preferences panel to edit how long the computer has to be in sleep mode before asking for the password. This can prove a quite useful feature.

57. Google and Yahoo! calendars. If you have something planned on your Google or/and Yahoo! calendars, it can be a good idea to import them into Snow Leopard. Add a new account under the iCall preferences, select the server and you are done.

58. Upload YouTube clips from QuickTime X. If you want to upload a clip to YouTube, open a video with QuickTime X and press Share on the menu bar. The same menu will enable you to upload movies to MobileMe and convert movies so you can send them to iTunes.

59. Video capture with QuickTime X. You don't need any other application to capture video from the iSight camera, a FireWire camera or an audio input of your choice. You can also choose to record your screen and save it as a movie.

60. Snow Leopard tells you what application is using the drive so you can't eject it. This is way better than the "busy" warning in Leopard.

61. In Snow Leopard, the trash will look more like Windows's Recycle Bin, meaning you can simply click "Put Back" to restore the item to its original location.

62. Time-Zone Detection feature. No matter where you may be in the world, Snow Leopard can detect your location via Wi-Fi hotspots and adjust the clock and the time zone to match your movement.

63. Snow Leopard allows you to use the trackpad to enter Chinese characters into a text application by pressing Control+Shift+Space.

64. Snow Leopard is a 64-bit operating system, but it defaults to 32-bit mode to maintain compatibility with print drivers and other software that haven't been upgraded yet. To take full advantage of Snow Leopard's speed, you'll want to run in 64-bit mode.

65. Mail Event Invitations. When you receive a mail from a friend that invites you to a certain event, giving you the date, iCal will be able to create a new event on your calendar by putting together the information from the message. Thus, you event will automatically show the date and the location if you accept the invitation.

66. Sticky Notes Shortcuts. Probably as a reply to Windows 7's sticky notes, Apple managed to improve what Microsoft first brought on the market. The cool thing is that you can assign a keyboard shortcut for creating a sticky note with the text you have selected. To set the shortcut, go to System Preferences -> Keyboard).

67. Zoom by touching the trackpad. A cool feature is that you can make the Desktop icons bigger or smaller by pinching the trackpad. If you extend, it will zoom out, if you pinch, it will zoom in. Very fast and very useful when your Desktop gets too crowded.

68. Preview Image Importing. There is no need to go to the Image Capture screen just to import photos and edit them. With Snow Leopard, this can be done from Preview.

69. When troubleshooting Mac OS X, you can boot in safe mode, which loads the bare minimum necessary to run Mac OS X. This will let you boot up and correct any problems caused by drivers or other programs that normally start automatically. To boot in safe mode, hold down the Shift key after restarting or shutting down and booting back up again.

70. Control+F2 – Highlights the Apple Menu. Now you can use the arrow keys to highlight different menu titles (such as File or Edit) or menu commands (such as Print or Edit). Then press Return to choose an option.

71. Control+F3 – Highlights the Dock. Now you can use the left/right arrow keys to highlight icons on the Dock and press Return to select a program to run.

72. Single-click on all the various labels of an address card to get a variety of options, depending on what you click on.

73. It's very easy to make a group mailing list. But don't send e-mail to a list of people unless you know everyone on that list wants to receive that mail.

74. If you want to burn music CDs, use iTunes: First create a Playlist in iTunes, then insert a blank CD-R, and burn the Playlist to the CD-R.

75. To deselect an icon, just click anywhere else, preferably on a blank spot on your Desktop.

76. To instantly re-size your window to the size it was previously, single-click the green button.

77. If you are in the process of moving the mouse and you run out of room, while continuing to hold the mouse button down, pick up the mouse, move it over, and keep going.

78. If your mouse or keyboard ever stops working, the first thing to do is unplug the item and plug it back in again—that almost always kicks it into working.

79. If you accidentally double-click on an icon that is not a folder, it will open that application. To quit, click once on the menu to the right of the blue apple, slide your mouse down to the bottom and click once on Quit.

80. To minimize an open window in slow motion, hold the Shift key when you click on the yellow button or when you click on a window icon in the Dock.

81. Everything in a Finder window uses a single click, except when you want to open a folder icon into the window pane.

82. Only type one space after periods or any other punctuation.

83. The paper in the Trash icon is visual clue that there is something in the Trash.

84. The command to Close will close just that active window, it does not close the application.

85. The command to Quit will quit the active application. If you have unsaved documents still open, you will be asked if you want to save them first.

86. Click on F1 on the keyboard to reduce the brightness of the display one step at a time.

87. You can use Spotlight to locate files within Time Machine.

88. Mac Os X automatically associates most types of video files with QuickTime Player, so you can also open a video file by double-clicking it in a Finder window.

89. You can't change a user account when that user is logged in with another session (on a Mac that uses Fast User Switching).

90. Once you encrypt your files with FileVault, the only way to retrieve your files is with a password. If you forget or lose your password, you have effectively lost your files.

91. Pressing Control+Eject displays the Shutdown dialog giving you a choice of shutting down, restarting, or putting your Mac to sleep.

92. The link speed shown in Network Utility is the maximum speed of the link. The actual speed you get for data transfer will often be lower.

93. A share or network share is a folder or drive on a computer on your network that has been deliberately shared by the user or administrator so that you can access it.

94. When connecting to a folder shared on another computer, you need to enter your user name and password for that computer, not the name and password for your Mac user account.

95. After selecting Log Out... from the Apple Menu, instead of clicking the Log Out button, you can wait 60 seconds, and Mac OS X will log you out automatically.

96. Safari keeps a history of the Web pages you visit so that you can easily return to a site you've visited.

97. When Mail is running, its Dock icon displays a red circle showing the number of messages you've received but haven't read yet.

98. The easiest video camera to use with iChat is Apple's iSight, which comes built into consumer desktop Macs and all laptop Macs.

99. You can execute whatever feature you put in an active screen corner by simply moving the mouse to that corner until the mouse pointer disappears.

100. Depending on the updates you're installing, you may have need to agree to a license agreement.

101. Since sending e-mail with a Mac is so easy, stay in touch with all of your distant family members.

PART 8

The Internet

The Internet

The Internet is a worldwide network of computers. In a network, computers "talk" with each other electronically and allow you to gather or share information from around the world.

Two types of computers make up the Internet: servers and clients. Servers store data (information, pictures, files, etc.) and serve it upon request, to computers known as clients. The Internet connects millions of servers and clients around the world.

The Internet is often referred to as The Net, The Information Superhighway, Cyberspace or The World Wide Web (www).

World Wide Web

The World Wide Web is a system of accessing information on the Internet. It is the graphical, multimedia portion of the Internet.

The Web links one Internet site to another with hypertext links. With hypertext links, you click on words that are highlighted in a passage and jump to a new location where more information on that subject is provided.

Do not expect every resource on the Internet to be accessible via the Web. To be accessible, a document must be coded with links that can be read by Web servers. E-mail and newsgroups are on the Internet, but are not part of the Web.

Getting Online

To get online, you will need:

- Your computer turned on.
- A way to connect to the Internet: cable, satellite, DSL, IDSN or telephone connection.
- An Internet Service Provider (ISP) account.
- And a Web browser.

If you are going to use your telephone line to hook up to the Internet, you will need to have a dial-up modem. Most PCs come with a dial-up modem, but Macs do not. Therefore if you have a Mac, you will need to purchase a dial-up modem. Apple makes the Mac without a dial-up modem because more and more people are getting broadband connections since they are faster.

Getting Connected

Your best options are cable, DSL or satellite access. These are known as broadband connections. They offer high speeds for a fixed monthly charge. Call your local cable TV operator/DSL provider/satellite dish provider to find out if it is available in your area.

Another way to connect is by using a modem and dialing-up through the standard telephone system. This is the cheapest, but slowest way to connect.

If using a dial-up, a second phone line dedicated for computer use can be very beneficial. If you only have one phone line, you cannot use the phone if the computer is online. With the expense of a second line, it might be cheaper, easier and faster to get a broadband connection.

Internet Service Provider (ISP)

An Internet Service Provider (ISP) is an entity that has the communications and computer facilities that let you connect to its Internet link. Usually there is a fee for this service.

Sometimes the ISP is referred to as the host or server. A server makes files available to other computers. The client, your computer, uses software so you can perform online functions.

There are many ISPs from which to choose. There are local, national and international providers. The local providers are usually independent and may limit their services to Internet access and e-mail. National and international providers may offer not only Internet access and e-mail, but also many members-only services and content. When looking for a provider, consider if they provide easy access to resources, services and information that is of greatest interest to you. All providers are not equal.

Switching Online Services

You are under no obligation to stick with the first ISP you try. That is unless you have a contract for service. Then you must adhere to the terms of your contract. Just like cell phone service, there might be an early termination fee if you have a specified length of service contract.

We have used a dial-up ISP, a satellite ISP and a DSL provider--- all different companies. We found that every time we increased the speed of our Internet connection, the happier we were.

Software For Accessing The Internet

Usually your ISP provides the necessary software and hardware to connect to the Internet. If your provider does not provide free software, maybe they are not the best provider choice.

Once you have established an account and connection, you are free to use whatever browser you want to, and whatever e-mail client that the ISP supports.

Web Browser

A web browser is the key piece of Internet software needed to access and navigate the Web. The interface enables you to ask for and view web pages.

Your computer will come with a web browser. In addition, most ISPs supply a customized browser as part of their Internet package. But you do not have to use the ISP's prepackaged browser.

Some popular browsers are Apple Safari, Google Chrome, Mozilla Firefox and Microsoft Internet Explorer. You can have more than one browser on your computer. Or, you can try them all and choose the one that suits you best.

Domain Name

A domain name identifies and locates a host computer or service on the Internet. It is the identifying title given to a system of computers. It is registered in much the same way as a company name.

The most popular domain types are usually one of the following:

.com = Company or commercial concern.

.edu = Educational institutions.

.gov = Government body.

.mil = Military site.

.net = Internet gateway or administrative host.

.org = Non-profit organization.

Because the Internet is growing rapidly, new domain suffixes have been created. Others include .info, .biz, .tv, .us, .cc, .name, .bz, .co. More will be added as needed. Countries may also have their own suffix. For example, .jp is Japan and .ca is Canada.

Logging On To The Internet

You are ready to log-on if you have a computer, a broadband ISP, all of your connections have been made and you open your Web browser.

If you only have a dial-up ISP, you will need an internal/external modem, you will need to dial out and connect to your ISP and then you can open your browser. You can also set up your computer to dial out automatically whenever an Internet demand program is opened (Web browser or e-mail client).

Web Page

A web page is a document on the Web. Web pages can include text, pictures, graphics, animations, video and audio. They may also contain links that connect you to other web pages.

Different locations on the Web are known as websites. A website is comprised of one or more web pages.

Home Page

The first page of a website is often called the home page. It is the primary web page for an individual, software application or organization.

Home page also has another meaning. It refers to the page that appears when you start your browser and acts as your home base for exploring the Web.

Your ISP may by default have a home page in its browser software. However, you can have any web page as your home page. I have my local TV station's home page as my home page as that gives me top news stories, weather and an easy-to-use local search engine. Your ISP may have a similar set up that you can customize to your liking.

To change your home page:

- In Safari, click on its name in the Menu Bar, then click Preferences.
- In Internet Explorer, click on Tools, then Internet Options.
- In Firefox, click on Tools, then Options.
- Under the general tab of each, there is a space to type in the web page of your choice. To make the process easier, surf to the page you want, then click Use Current Page.

Hypertext Linking

Web pages are written in HTML code (HyperText Markup Language). They contain connections, links, to other web pages. These links are embedded within the text.

A hyperlink is a signpost to take you to other web pages with related information. The link appears as an icon, graphic, image or word in a file, that when clicked with the mouse, automatically takes you to another web page. A link is usually underlined or displayed in a different color. The mouse pointer turns into a "hand" to show that the icon, graphic, image or word is a link.

To pursue a link, click on the highlighted text or image. You will jump to the new web page. This may be in the current website, or you may be directed to a different website. You can always return to previous Web pages and sites by using the Back Button on the browser toolbar.

Uniform Resource Locator (URL)

A Uniform Resource Locator (URL) is a fancy term for a Web address. The URL system is a standardized addressing format for material accessible over the Internet. Each web page has a unique URL so that you can find any individual web page easily.

If you know a website's URL, you can go directly to it by typing the URL in the address field of your browser, then pressing Return (Enter).

Each URL has three parts: the protocol, the host name and the file path.

Reading from left to right identifies the domain and sub-domains within the site. The slashes are dividers that are necessary for the address. Do not insert any spaces. Example: http://www.theseniorsguide.com.

http, https

http stands for HyperText Transfer Protocol and refers to the set of rules used by your browser to access and display Web pages.

If you see the prefix https, it signifies a secure or encrypted version of http. Most online merchants, banks and brokerage houses use https as their communication method. This ensures your financial information is encrypted so others cannot read it.

www stands for the World Wide Web. This is the main avenue for information stored out on the Internet.

Although http (or https) and www are used in almost every address, all browsers are smart enough to know that. So instead of typing the entire address for our website in your browser, http://www.theseniorsguide.com, you can type theseniorsguide.com and you will still get to us.

Surfing The Web

You can browse, or surf the Web in several ways:

- You can open any web page by typing its address in the Address Bar of your web browser.
- When you are viewing a web page, you can surf to related sites by clicking the links on the page.
- You can also use toolbar buttons to move between pages, search the Internet, go back a page or forward a page or to refresh a page.
- You can use a search engine to find related web pages based on your inputs.

Searching For Information

To search the Web, you should use a search engine. A search engine is a program that allows you to locate specific information from online databases. There are a number of search engines to choose from and each has its own strengths. I'm sure you've heard of Google since they are the largest search company.

To search the Internet for anything, simply type in the topic in the search box and you will get results instantly. Type the word or phrase that describes what you are looking for. The search engine then displays Web pages that match your request.

Different search engines source, store and retrieve their data differently. Although Google is our favorite, others are HotBot, AltaVista, Yahoo!, Infoseek, Excite and Bing.

The search engine does a lot of work for you, but it cannot read minds. For example, if you put Levi's in the search box, hoping to find a new pair of blue jeans, don't be surprised if you get an essay on the history of indigo ink. The search engine looks for the keyword that you typed. If a web page has that word in it, the page will be displayed in the search results regardless of whether or not you really wanted to know about indigo ink.

So, to find a web page where you can purchase a pair of Levi's, you might want to search "purchase Levi's" and see what you get. Try different search parameters and you will get the hang of it quickly.

What If A Web Page Will Not Open?

It is just a matter of time before you click on a link or type in a Web address that does not work. There are a couple of reasons this might happen. If only one URL does not work, you know that it is a wrong address, the host at its end has a problem or the address has changed or been turned off. Addresses must be exact or you will not get the page that you are looking for.

If no URLs work, check to make sure you have an Internet connection. If you do not have a connection to the Internet, make sure all of your wiring is connected properly and that any external boxes are powered. If you still do not have an Internet connection, your ISP may be having technical difficulties. If you do have an Internet connection, but cannot connect to any website, close and reopen your browser. If you still cannot connect, try restarting your computer.

Web Address Error Codes

Some of the most common errors codes you might see are:

- Incorrect host name. When the address points to a non-existent host, your browser will return an error "Host not found". Most of the time this is due to a mistyped address.
- Illegal domain name. The illegal host name is mostly due to wrong punctuation in an address. For example, a single slash (/) instead of two (//) or forgetting to put a dot after www.
- Page not found. If a file has moved, changed names or you have overlooked capitalization, you will get a message from the server telling you the file does not exist.
- Host refuses entry. The host is either overloaded with traffic or temporarily off-limits.

Downloading

When you download a file, you are retrieving information from an online service onto your computer. When requested, the online service sends you a copy of the file. To start this process:

- Right-click on the link.
- Select Download File and follow the prompts, if any.
- You can also use the File menu in the Menu Bar and save a web page with the Save As command. When a file is made available simply so that you can download it, you can click on it and it will download.

Uploading

Uploading is the process of putting a file onto a website. If you are planning on uploading files, you will need a FTP (File Transfer Protocol) program. These specialized programs are usually not included with your computer.

Uploading a file is different from sending a file to someone via e-mail. Uploading transfers the file or files to a server where they are stored. Sending a file or files to someone via e-mail sends the person a copy of your file, or files, which they then have on their computer.

Keeping Track Of Your Favorite Websites

You can keep track of your favorite websites via the Bookmark function in Safari, Chrome and Firefox, or Favorites in Internet Explorer.

You should organize your bookmarks list right from the beginning. If not, it might be hard to find an individual bookmark from a long list. Create folders in the bookmark list to hold similar websites.

Newsgroups

A newsgroup is an online discussion or forum group, dealing with a wide range of topics. It is an electronic bulletin board of messages. People from all over the world can post or respond to other peoples' messages. You can start new discussions any time you want to.

Each newsgroup is focused on a particular topic. Usenet consists of over 25,000 different newsgroups.

To access and review newsgroup postings, you need a newsreader. Once you have a newsreader, you have to subscribe to a newsgroup so that messages are automatically downloaded into your inbox. Newsgroups are never private. Make sure you do not say anything that you would not mind seeing on the front page of your newspaper the next day.

Chat Rooms

Chat rooms are the equivalent of meeting rooms in which you carry on live keyboard conversations with everyone in the room as a group or with particular individuals.

Do you remember your mother telling you not to talk to strangers? Well, unless you already know the people in a chat room, they are all strangers. So be careful. Never reveal any financial or personal information in a chat room. And, if you do not want to read about it in tomorrow's newspaper, do not talk about it in the chat room.

Some security issues associated with chat rooms have been removed by instant messaging. Instant messaging takes place amongst people on a 'buddy list'. Only people you put on your buddy list will be there.

Web Mail

Web mail is e-mail that you look at with a web browser, rather than an e-mail program. Your ISP has to support Web mail and give you that option. Web mail only works when you are online and using a browser to go to the ISP's Web mail Web pages. Once you are at the Web mail page, all the normal e-mail functions are available to you, but all resident on your ISP's server. This means you can use any computer, anywhere to connect to your e-mail account. This is very handy if you are traveling without your computer. To use Web mail, you will need to know the Web address for your ISP's Web mail function, your account name and password. Once logged in, you can do all of your e-mail work online. We will get into the specifics of e-mail in the next part of the book.

Plug-Ins

A plug-in is a small auxiliary program that works with your browser. It is a script, utility or a set of instructions that add to the functionality of a program without changing the program's base code. Plug-ins work seamlessly with your browser and only when needed.

If you are surfing the Web and come across a website that requires a plug-in you do not have, you most likely will be offered to download the plug-in right then. After you download and install it, your browser will call on it when it needs it.

Examples of plug-ins are RealPlayer and Flash. RealPlayer is an audio plug-in for Internet based audio and video. Flash enables multimedia effects that are written into a website.

Cookies

A cookie is information from a website sent to the browser and stored on your hard drive so the website can retrieve it later. It is a digital I.D. Card. Each time you revisit that website, it will actually know your individual browser. Most websites routinely log your visit. The cookie contains information that is recorded against your IP (Internet Protocol) address.

You have the option to allow your browser to accept, or reject cookies. Some websites require your computer to accept cookies if you want to take full advantage of the website. If you need to go to that site, you will have to accept cookies.

Security On The Internet

Never give out personal or financial information unless you absolutely know the website you are working with. Try not to use links to business websites from e-mails. Type in the real address in your Web browser instead of cutting and pasting the link. Sometimes crooks make a convincing e-mail look like it is from a legitimate business entity.

A secure server encrypts your information. That means that the information has been scrambled by software to make it unreadable by anyone but the receiving computer. Always make sure your financial transactions are done over a secure server.

Web browsers Safari, Firefox and Internet Explorer include security features that let you know when your connection is secure and when it is not. A secure site is denoted with a locked padlock in the bottom bar of the browser window.

Be careful out there. Keep in mind that digital information is easily manipulated. Do not give out any information unless you know the receiver. Be a smart shopper.

Never give your passwords to anyone over the Internet.

Bad Stuff On The Internet

There is information out there that everyone is happy to see, and information that you never want to see. However, there are many more safe sites than unsafe sites.

The Internet allows people to meet without face-to-face contact. Wherever people congregate, there always seems to be a few bad apples in the barrel.

It is possible to block access to certain sites which are inappropriate for children. Using the Parental Control features in your computer, you can filter out a lot of the bad stuff not only for children, but for yourself. You do not have to look at anything you do not want to. A lot of the bad stuff can be blocked at the server level.

Viruses

A virus is an unwanted file or set of instructions that attaches itself to files in a computer system, usually causing harm to a computer. It replicates itself as the file is shared from computer to computer. The most likely mode of transmission is via e-mail attachments. Viruses are not naturally occurring bugs. People who want to cause havoc in the computer world create them. Other forms of malicious software include Spyware, Malware and Adware.

Ending An Internet Session

To end an Internet session, log out from a password protected website and simply close your browser.

If you have a dial-up Internet connection, and if you have not set up your browser to automatically dial-up when you open your browser, you will need to manually turn off the modem.

25 Internet Tips And Tricks

1. Know who you're dealing with. If the company is unfamiliar, check with your state or local consumer protection agency and the Better Business Bureau. Some websites have feedback forums, which can provide useful information about other people's experiences with particular sellers. Get the physical address and phone number in case there is a problem.

2. Look for information about how complaints are handled. It can be difficult to resolve complaints, especially if the seller or charity is located in another country. Look on the website for information about programs the company or organization participates in that require it to meet standards for reliability and help to handle disputes.

3. Be aware that no complaints is no guarantee. Fraudulent operators open and close quickly, so the fact that no one has made a complaint yet doesn't meant that the seller or charity is legitimate. You still need to look for other danger signs of fraud.

4. Don't believe promises of easy money. If someone claims that you can earn money with little or no work, get a loan or credit card even if you have bad credit, or make money with little or no risk, it's likely a scam.

5. Resist pressure. Legitimate companies and charities will be happy to give you time to make a decision. It's probably a scam if they demand that you act immediately or won't take "No" for an answer.

6. Think twice before entering contests operated by unfamiliar companies. Fraudulent marketers sometimes use contest entry forms to identify potential victims.

7. Be cautious about unsolicited e-mails. They are often fraudulent. If you are familiar with the company or charity that sent you the e-mail and you don't want to receive further messages, send a reply asking to be removed from the

e-mail list. However, responding to unknown senders may simply verify that yours is a working e-mail address and result in even more unwanted messages from strangers. The best approach may simply be to delete the e-mail.

8. Beware of imposters. Someone might send you an e-mail pretending to be connected with a business or charity, or create a website that looks just like that of a well-known company or charitable organization. If you're not sure that you're dealing with the real thing, find another way to contact the legitimate business or charity and ask.

9. Guard your personal information. Don't provide your credit card or bank account number unless you are actually paying for something. Your social security number should not be necessary unless you are applying for credit. Be especially suspicious if someone claiming to be from a company with whom you have an account asks for information that the business already has.

10. Beware of "dangerous downloads." In downloading programs to see pictures, hear music, play games, etc., you could download a virus that wipes out your computer files or connects your modem to a foreign telephone number, resulting in expensive phone charges. Only download programs from websites you know and trust.

11. Pay the safest way. Credit cards are the safest way to pay for online purchases because you can dispute the charges if you never get the goods or services or the offer was misrepresented. Federal law limits your liability to $50 if someone makes unauthorized charges to your account.

12. When adding images to your web pages, you should use GIF or JPEG images. These are the most popular types of images on the Web.

13. Each web browser will display your web pages in a slightly different way.

14. A bounced message is a message that returns to you because it cannot reach its destination.

15. If you choose a DSL or cable Internet account, the phone company or cable company usually supplies the modem. If you choose a dial-up account you have to get our own modem.

16. Pages with large pictures or a lot of content are sometimes slow to load; sometimes the net itself is just slow. Also, when things seem to be so slow that you suspect they've stopped, your network connection may have gone down (perhaps your phone is disconnected, or your Internet software needs to be restarted, or your Internet service provider is down).

17. Try to avoid a lot of clicking ahead; clicking over and over on a spot won't make the page load any faster, and will make it slower.

18. If you click on a link before a page has finished loading, you will interrupt the transfer of data. Then, the links going to later places within that page won't all work, and the computer won't tell you why. At this point, reload the page; to do this, click on the "reload" or "refresh" button.

19. Some pages no longer exist. When this is the case, you'll usually get a message telling you that the file was not found. At this point, going back to the previous page (using the "Back" button) is the easiest option.

20. Take advantage of online banking, investing, and bill pay. It's safe and saves you time.

21. Choose a home page that gives you the information you need. Yahoo! and MSN are great choices.

22. Don't forget to empty your Trash in your e-mail client. Messages stick around until you do.

23. Choose the fastest Internet connection you can afford. Faster speeds make a difference.

24. Let virus software scan your system every day.

25. Download large PDF files and read them. Reading them online is very slow.

PART 9

E-mail

E-mail

E-mail is short for electronic mail. It is digital correspondence, sent via the Internet.

E-mail gives you the ability to send and receive text messages to or from anyone with an e-mail address, anywhere in the world. You can include other files, pictures, audio or video through the use of attachments to your e-mail.

E-mail is more like a conversation than a formal correspondence. It is a speedy way to get a message to someone, for free. It should be concise, to the point and well written. Do not forget to check your spelling, grammar and punctuation. Your teachers were right. Spelling counts!

How Does E-mail Work?

Assuming you have an Internet Service Provider (ISP) and an Internet connection, you simply create a letter in your e-mail program. When you select Send Mail, your e-mail is sent via your ISP's server to the server where your recipient has their e-mail account. When they retrieve their mail, they get your message along with any others that may have been sent to them.

When someone sends you a message, that message is sent to your ISP and stored there. When you log on and check your e-mail, the message is downloaded into your mail program.

As we mentioned in the Internet Part, you can also use Web mail if your ISP supports that function. With Web mail, you do not download the e-mail into your e-mail program to view it. You view your e-mail as you would any web page. If you delete an e-mail from your Web mail account, it is gone. However, if you leave the message on the server, the next time you use your e-mail program at home, the e-mail will be downloaded to your computer and deleted from the server.

Getting Started

As far as software goes, you will need an e-mail client. Windows XP and Vista, and Apple's Mac come with e-mail programs already installed (Outlook Express, Windows Mail and Mail respectively). With Windows 7, you will need to download the e-mail program from Microsoft. It is part of the Windows Live suite of applications. It's a free download so you don't have to worry about buying another program.

When you first start your e-mail program, you will be asked to set up your e-mail account. (If you have not established an account with an ISP, do that first.) You will need to know your account name, password, e-mail address, SMTP and POP settings and any SSL settings your ISP may use. Fill in the required information and you are good to go.

E-mail Address

Your ISP manages the e-mail address system used in its accounts. You can pick your user name, but the server name will be assigned by the ISP.

The first part of the address, before the @ symbol, is the user name. You generally get to pick your user name. So long as no one else at the ISP has chosen it, it is yours. The second part, or the domain name, defines the ISP, or business name, where the e-mail servers are located. Those two parts are separated by the @ sign (pronounced "at").

The domain name is followed by an extension that indicates the type of organization to which the network belongs.

Here is an example of an e-mail address:

Rebecca@theseniorsguide.com

Writing And Sending E-mail

First, open your e-mail program. Then click Compose New Message. This may be listed in a drop down menu titled New. This will open a new blank e-mail message. In the To: line, put the recipient's address. In the Subject: line, give your e-mail a title. In the composition section, write your e-mail.

Make sure you are online, then click Send. That's it. Your note is going to the other person at the speed of light.

If you have more than one e-mail account, another line will give you the choice of which account will be shown for the From: account.

Receiving E-mail

Make sure you are online. Open your e-mail program. Then click Get Mail. That's it. If your e-mails have large files attached to them, the download can take a few minutes. With Windows 7, you click on Sync which will retrieve all of your e-mails from the server.

Using The Address Book

Within just about every e-mail program resides an address book. This is a handy place to store all of the e-mail addresses you collect. If an address is in the address book, when you start typing a name in the To: section of an e-mail address, the address book will try to give you choices of addresses that match what you are typing. When you see the name of the person you want to send your e-mail to, just click the name and they will be entered into the To: line.

You can ask the address book to log the name and address of people who you respond to with e-mail. This can be turned on in the Preferences section of the address book in Apple Mail, and under the Tools menu, Options and then the Send tab in Windows Mail. This makes it easy to log the addresses of people you want to write to in the future.

E-mail Shortcuts

When you start typing an e-mail address or name in the To: line, Mail shows you a list of addresses or names that contain what you have typed so far. You can then select from that list which saves you keystrokes and from having to remember addresses.

Mailing Lists

You can create mailing lists from your address book. This is a list of people with a common characteristic that you want to use, such as 'Greeting Card' or 'Block Party'.

When you want to send a message to an entire group of people, simply address the e-mail to the group's name. Everyone on that list will get a copy of the message.

This works whether you are using the To:, CC: or BCC: lines.

Replying To An E-mail

To reply to an e-mail message:

- Make sure the message is selected in the list or click on the header to open it.
- Click the Reply, or Reply All button. This will automatically copy the original message and address it back to the sender, if you have your Preferences set up this way. (This is a good idea so that whatever you write can be referenced to the original message.)
- Type your message.
- Click Send.

The Reply button will send your message to the person who sent you the original e-mail. The Reply All button will send a copy of your reply to everyone in the To:, CC: and BCC: lists. Try not to use Reply All unless everyone on the list really needs to see your message. For example, if your cousin sends out jokes to a big mailing list, not everyone in the list needs to know what you thought of the joke. On the other hand, if they sent out a message asking for your opinion on a political topic, you may want to share your thoughts with everyone on the list.

Forwarding An E-mail

To forward an e-mail you received to someone else, simply click the Forward button, put the person's name you want to forward to in the To: line, add any comments you want to make and then click Send.

To help combat spam and the spread of viruses, and to help make sure forwarded e-mails do not get blocked by anti-spam software, or deleted without reading by the recipient, we recommend that you always add a note at the beginning of a forwarded e-mail. This gives the recipient a better idea that this came from a real person that they know, vice an infected computer from somewhere in the world.

Carbon Copies And Blind Carbon Copies

If you want to send two or more people the same message, and you do not mind if they know who else is receiving it, type all of the names in the To: line or, type the primary person in the To: line and everyone else in the CC: line. Use a comma to separate the names in the list.

To send an e-mail without disclosing anyone on your mailing list, put yourself in the To: line, and everyone else in the BCC: line. When you put someone's name in the BCC: line their name and address is masked from all others. However, anyone, including those in the BCC list can see who is in the To: and CC: fields.

If you do not see the BCC: line when you start a new message, with Apple Mail, click the little box to the left of the Subject: line. A small list of fields will pop up. Make sure there is a check mark by bcc. With Windows 7, there is a note to the right of the subject line that will reveal the CC and BCC lines.

Sending An Attachment

Sending attachments is easy. When you are ready to attach a photo or document to your message, place the cursor where you want the attachment to show up in your message, generally at the end of your message. Click the Attach button. That is the button with the paperclip on it. Then browse to the file you want to attach and click Choose File.

If you are a Mac user, and you know you are sending an attachment to a Windows computer, make sure there is a check mark in the box that says Send Windows Friendly Attachments.

Opening An Attachment

To help combat viruses, you should never 'just open' an attachment. Mail gives you two tools to check out attachments to see whether or not you should save them and open them.

The first tool is the little arrow to the left of the attachment line. Click that and you will see the details of the attachment. Next, you can use the Quick Look button to preview the attachment without using an application.

When you determine you want to open the attachment, just click on it. If you have the software type that created the attachment, it will open.

If you want to save the attachment to your Mac, click the Save button that is next to the Quick Look button.

Is E-mail Private?

No. E-mail is never confidential. Without encryption, the possibility exists that e-mail can be accessed and read by others.

In addition, although you may send an e-mail to just one person, they can forward it to others. Do not send anything that you would not mind reading on the front page of your local newspaper the next day. It's amazing how fast things spread via the Internet and digital technology.

E-mail Etiquette

While online, you should always practice good social skills and behavior. Since you will often be communicating with people you do not know well, or cannot tell what your mood is at the moment, you should always follow some basic rules.

No SHOUTING. Typing in all upper case signifies shouting. You can use upper case for emphasis in a word or two. ANY MORE THAN THAT AND YOU'RE SHOUTING!!!!!

No flaming. When another online person posts an opinion that you think is outrageous or ridiculous, do not respond with excessive outrage. Keep your temper and language under control.

No spamming. Do not post the same message to hundreds of newsgroups. Do not forward mail in bulk to everyone in your contacts list. Be selective in what you forward and who you forward it to.

Save your humor and jokes for good friends and close confidants. Humor can be easily misinterpreted. One person's joke is another person's spam.

If you are going to forward something, take the time to take out all of the extraneous addressing from previous posters of the message. For example, I once had a message that came forwarded from 30 previous people, each using the attachment feature to send the joke. If just one person had taken the time to remove all of the previous forwards and had just sent the joke, I would have enjoyed it more.

Part 6 Mini Index

Part 7 Mini Index

Part 8 Mini Index

Part 9 Mini Index

101 Favorite Websites

1.	The Senior's Guide Series	www.TheSeniorsGuide.com
2.	MeAndMyCaregiver(s), Inc.	www.MeAndMyCaregivers.com
3.	Looking for WW2 MIAs	www.BentProp.org
4.	One Look Online Dictionary	www.onelook.com
5.	MapQuest	www.mapquest.com
6.	National Caregiving Institute	www.NationalCaregivingInstitute.org
7.	Bored	www.bored.com
8.	The bunk stops here!	www.purportal.com
9.	USPS Zipcode+4 Lookup	http://zip4.usps.com/zip4
10.	U.S. Government's Official Web Site	www.usa.gov
11.	Get your mail from POP3 Accounts	www.mail2web.com
12.	Online Almanac	www.infoplease.com
13.	Internet Movie Database	www.imdb.com
14.	Internet Public Library	www.ipl.org
15.	Price Watch	www.pricewatch.com
16.	How Things Work	www.howstuffworks.com
17.	World History	www.hyperhistory.com
18.	Fodor's Travel Guides	www.fodors.com
19.	Virtual Reference Desk	www.itools.com
20.	The Why Files	www.whyfiles.org
21.	Genealogy	www.ancestry.com
22.	Golf Courses	www.golfcourse.com
23.	Web Solutions	www.R3WebSolutions.com
24.	AARP	www.aarp.org
25.	Baby Boomer's Headquarters	www.bbhq.com

26.	Habitat for Humanity	www.habitat.org
27.	Jewish Information Center	www.jewishnet.net
28.	Romeo Computers	www.romeocomp.com
29.	WW2 MIA	www.bentprop.org
30.	Astrology	www.astrologyzone. com
31.	Reiki Healing	www.samarasays.com
32.	The Smithsonian Institute	www.si.edu
33.	Museum of Natural History	www.amnh.org
34.	The Kentucky Horse Park	www.imh.org
35.	The National Corvette Museum	www.corvettemuseum.com
36.	San Diego Aerospace Museum	www.AerospaceMuseum.org
37.	Veterans News/Information Source	www.vnis.com
38.	AAA Online	www.aaa.com
39.	U.S. Postal Service	www.usps.gov
40.	Britannica Online	www.eb.com
41.	Interesting Videos	www.youtube.com
42.	Kelly Blue Book	www.kbb.com
43.	Social Security Online	www.ssa.gov
44.	Kiplinger Online	www.kiplinger.com
45.	Investment FAQs	www.invest-faq.com
46.	NASDAQ	www.nasdaq.com
47.	Cancer Nutrition Info	www.cancernutritioninfo.com
48.	Digital Photography	www.fickr.com
49.	Fashion	www.zoomzoom.com
50.	Food 411	www.food411.com
51.	Home Improvement	www.digitalhome.cnet.com

52.	Life Expectancy Calculator	www.livingto100.com.
53.	Pets	www.dogster.com
54.	Social Networking	www.ineighbors.org
55.	Travel Bookings	www.sidestep.com
56.	Classifieds	www.craigslist.org
57.	Comparison Shopping	www.shopzilla.com.
58.	Deal of the Day	www.woot.com
59.	Kitsch	www.mcphee.com
60.	Shoes	www.zappos.com
61.	When Things Go Wrong	www.complaints.com
62.	TV News	www.blinkxtv.com
63.	Consumer Protection	www.idtheftcenter.org.
64.	General Reference	www.answers.com
65.	Legal Matters	www.findlaw.com
66.	Politics	www.publicagenda.org
67.	Web Search	www.clusty.com.
68.	Animation	www.aardman.com
69.	Books	www.complete-review.com
70.	Classical Music	www.opus1classical.com
71.	Galleries	www.coudal.com/moom.php
72.	Games	www.orisinal.com
73.	Humor	www.mcsweeneys.net
74.	More Funny Stuff	www.zefrank.com
75.	Podcasting	www.podcastbunker.com.
76.	Radio	www.mercora.com
77.	Television	www.tv.com

78.	Forbes	www.forbes.com
79.	Elder Law Answers	www.McDermott.elderlawanswers.com
80.	Bingo	www.bingozone.com
81.	Friend Finder	www.meetasenior.com
82.	Medical Info	www.webmd.com
83.	Welcome to the White House	www.whitehouse.gov
84.	National Hospice Organization	www.nho.org
85.	American Cancer Society	www.cancer.org
86.	Ask the Dietician	www.dietician.com
87.	Administration on Aging	www.aoa.gov
88.	Wine	www.wine.com
89.	Classic Cars	www.classiccar.com
90.	Recipes	www.epicurious.com
91.	American Kennel Club	www.aka.org
92.	National Public Radio	www.npr.org
93.	NASCAR	www.nascar.com
94.	Movies	www.movies.com
95.	Hotels	www.hotels.com
96.	Ice cream	www.benjerrys.com
97.	Sleep	www.sleepnet.com
98.	American Contract Bridge	www.acbl.org
99.	Yahoo!	www.yahoo.com
100.	Weather	www.weather.com
101.	Computer Help	www.theseniorsguide.com